The
Immigrants Speak

Carol Kentle
1985

The
Immigrants Speak

Italian Americans Tell Their Story

by Salvatore J. LaGumina

1979
CENTER FOR MIGRATION STUDIES
NEW YORK

The Center for Migration Studies is an educational non-profit institute founded in New York in 1964 to encourage and facilitate the study of sociological, demographic, historical, legislative and pastoral aspects of human migration and ethnic group relations. The opinions expressed in this work are those of the authors.

The Immigrants Speak

Second Edition
Copyright © 1981

Center for Migration Studies
209 Flagg Place
Staten Island, New York 10304

ISBN 0-913256-37-4
Library of Congress Catalog Number: 79-67388
Printed in the United States of America

DEDICATED TO
TWO WOMEN

My mother, Maria La Gumina, who in her own life experience exemplifies the soul and the selflessness of the Italian immigrant.

and

My wife, Julia La Gumina, who was a constant source of love and encouragement while I completed the volume.

Preface

With the exception of deeply perceptive novels and plays, few other forms of verbal expression tell more about the human condition than the spoken and written records we call autobiography. The first-person histories which have been skillfully edited for inclusion in this volume not only mirror the psychology and personality of their authors but also provide a valuable insight into the Italian American immigration experience over the past century and are bound to interest the scholar as well as the general reader.

Moreover, these personal histories also help to humanize a field of study which has tended to become increasingly dehumanized with the rise of computer studies and the proliferation of quantitative analyses. Apparently, Professor LaGumina asked the right questions and managed to win the confidence of his subjects, for they emerge, not as sociological robots, but as flesh and blood individuals speaking their own minds, talking out of their own experiences. In doing so, they expand our awareness of what happened to Italian immigrants as they went about the business of adjusting to an alien society whose values often clashed with their own.

Responding perhaps to the all-too-prevalent cliche that Italian Americans are a mass of blue-collar workers and ultra conservatives, Professor LaGumina wisely directed his attention to both men and women of different occupations, social status, and political persuasions. There are coal miners and ditch-diggers (one of them from Sardinia helped to dig the Panama Canal), shoemakers (one of them, Remigio Pane, became a distinguished Professor at Rutgers University), teachers, a self-taught man of letters, a social worker, an artist, and a lawyer. In the course of learning their stories we also learn a great deal about Italian Americans they knew in occupations other than their own.

I was especially taken with the personal history of the late Joseph Zappulla, described by Professor LaGumina as a 'giant in Italian American letters although barely five feet tall'. The author of plays, short stories, essays and radio scripts, his work appeared in almost every major

Italian language periodical in this country. His experiences as a professional writer whose career spanned a half century provide us with an engrossing survey of the Italian American press. Zappulla was mainly a poet, who made his living as a journalist. With an artistry that makes us realize what a pity it is that his poems and short stories are known only to a limited Italian American audience, he includes in his account an unforgettably poignant visit to his dying mother in Sicily after their separation of thirty-one years.

Some of the outstanding accounts in this text are by women. Elvira Adorno, who had a long career as a high school teacher of Italian, depicts a family odyssey dominated by a clever father who, before being financially ruined by the depression of the 1930s, had developed a prosperous business producing hand-sewn flags. In a style that has literary grace, Bruna Pieracci, whose family migrated from the Northern Appenines to Iowa, graphically describes the harshness of life in a mining camp. Clara Grillo, a second generation Italian American, is marvelously observant as she combines the story of her domineering father with a fascinating account of what was going on in the Italian theater in Cleveland, Ohio, in the days when immigrants were grasping at any form of Italian nostalgia that would give them some respite from their non-Italian world.

To be sure, some of the accounts are more articulate and appealing than others. And a few express prejudices which may not sit well with certain readers (I, for one, bridled at the statement that Italians are incapable of governing themselves and badly need a strong man like Mussolini to take charge of their country). But whatever the virtues and deficiencies of the narrators, the quality they have in common which is omnipresent is honesty. It is to Professor LaGumina's credit that he was able to inspire his subjects to be themselves, without falling into such pitfalls as sentimentality and egoism. The result is a stunning mosaic of Italian Americana which, pleasurably, extends the boundaries of knowledge about America's largest white ethnic group.

The publication of this volume will, I hope, serve as an incentive to the publication of more life histories by Italian Americans, particularly of the quality and variety presented in this compilation.

Jerre Mangione
University of Pennsylvania
Philadelphia

Table of Contents

Foreword

Seeking to capitalize on the current preoccupation with self-identity and ethnic heritage, a major American airline has advertised, "Every American has two heritages". Similarly affected by popular approbation, the scholarly pursuit of "ethnicity" has also increased and has served to sensitize Americans to the diverse nationalities which have come to settle on American soil. This desire to fathom the "other" heritage has been instrumental in producing numerous written works on many ethnic groups and has, thereby, extended our knowledge of the nation as a whole.

Focusing on a single immigrant group to the United States, this volume seeks to further our understanding of Italian Americans, one of the nation's largest ethnic groups. Thus, rather than rely on the treatises of novelists, sociologists, historians, or other researchers, this volume relies on the ruminations, the feelings, the attitudes and the evaluations of the immigrants themselves, as they unfold for us the immigrant experience recalled by their personal life histories.

Personal autobiographical accounts as a sociological tool are neither novel nor unique to the study of Italian Americans. Notable among these are two full length volumes of recent publication, *Rosa, The Life of An Italian Immigrant,* by Marie Hall Ets, and *Polpetto*, by Frank Mele. There are also such outstanding novels on American Italian life as Pietro DiDonato's *Christ in Concrete* and Jerre Mangione's *Mount Allegro* which, although novel in form are, nevertheless, autobiographical. There have also been a number of article-length autobiographical accounts such as John Fante's "The Odyssey of a Wop", or Rocco Corresca's "The Biography of a Bootblack" to name only a few. Yet, despite these, no work has been written which permits a number of Italian Americans, from various occupations, to recount their experiences of emigration.

To initiate a response to this area of social research I proposed to undertake a number of interviews for this book. I am obliged to note that the idea was derived from the work by Henry Lucas entitled *Dutch Immigrant Memoirs and Selected Writings,* Vol. I. This work records accounts of many Dutch immigrants to America. It also depicts, however, the cost of assimilation to their new land. A careful reading of the accounts of the Dutch Americans reveals, I believe, that the personal autobiographical accounts of the immigrants record a wide range of experiences, which are usually lost in general historical or sociological treatments.

The accounts recorded in this volume, while undoubtedly susceptible to some theoretical categorization of the immigration process, nevertheless, demonstrate the individuality of the Italian immigrants in America's midst. These stories detail the lives of a people bridging two cultures in modern history. To learn about them is to take an important step in realizing what Italian immigrants of various backgrounds underwent in making the cultural transition and even more importantly it serves as a vehicle to understand and appreciate the making of American society.

The biographies in this collection have been selected from a larger number of individuals who were selected, contacted and interviewed, with the exception of two persons with whom communication was conducted by mail. The interviews revolved around a number of basic questions regarding emigration and assimilation into American life. The decision as to which individuals to interview was in a large part determined by communicating with people whom I had known or met through many years of interaction with and research about Italian Americans. The result of a career studying Italian Americans was the good fortune to make the acquaintance of many Americans of Italian descent whose biographies proved to be a fascinating source illuminating an almost distant portion of American history.

The list of interviews was supplemented by names suggested to me by colleagues in the same field of study and by friends and acquaintances. Consequently, after two years I had met with and conducted in-depth interviews with some three dozen people. Editorial and spatial exigencies precluded the inclusion of all of their stories, although each proved to be a rewarding learning experience. The autobiographies amount to a fair representation of a cross-section of Italian Americans. Most, but certainly not all, came from the typical working class background and although some continued their proletarian activities in this country, many clambered into the professions. Some led rather solitary, even lonely and heroic lives, while others became active participants in a variety of undertakings. As newcomers, they lived in the city's worst tenements and were exposed to the ravages of periodic epidemics. Some were exploited by absentee landlords, ruthless employers and even their fellow countrymen *padrones*. For the most part they toiled long hours at low wages, and many became victims of industrially related diseases.

The oldest of the interviewees emigrated to this country in what was considered the midst of the era of massive Italian emigration in the 1890s. At that time, the emigrating peoples came from a land which, although rich in history, had only recently achieved independent political unification in 1870 as the Papal States were joined to the remainder of Italy. The unification struggle under King Victor Emmanuel saw Italian peasants playing a minor role thereby explaining the relative absence of intense feeling for the movement on their part.

As a consequence of this belated political development, Italy was tardy in effecting the instruments of modern state administration. Centuries of misrule, of exploitation by outside powers as well as by domestic aristocracy and church hierarchy had left Italy far behind other western European countries whose economic, educational and social progress was much further advanced. Ironically, both the surviving aristocratic leadership and the emerging politicians failed to comprehend the severity of the crisis and the necessity to correct the country's internal problems.

Clearly Italy's history could not fail to affect the outlook of its people as did the nation's geographical and climatic circumstances. A formidable chain of mountains running the length of the Italian peninsula had served from time immemorial as an impassable barrier isolating the people, the villages, and dissecting the country. The mountains separated, moreover, northern Italy from other European countries, which meant that it would also be less influenced by movements beyond the Alps. Italy was blessed with few navigable rivers and its forest preserves had dwindled so precipitously that by mid-nineteenth century it constituted a major reason for an inadequate water supply. Malaria was a scourge from ancient Roman times and earthquakes were frequent ecological occurrences which proved disastrous to life and instrumental in producing a psychological sense of helplessness among its residents.

The population, while considerably homogeneous, had developed numerous distinctive language patterns or dialects, yet the Tuscan dialect served as the main unifying force. Unification did not bring an abrupt change to this division but it did serve to emphasize a north-south division replete with a northern exhibition of superiority toward the south.

Italy was an agricultural nation but its arid soil defied sound agricultural steps. In addition, the impact of deforestation meant that only a portion of land was arable (one-third in Sicily). Land ownership was characterized by a peculiar arrangement of *frazionamento,* a process of excessive land division, coupled with absentee landlordism and the perpetuation of obsolete methods. All of this served to inflict a low standard of living on a nation approaching near starvation conditions in some provinces as well as actual bread riots.

Given these conditions, it is no great wonder that emigration came to be regarded as a viable solution by multitudes. Indeed, Italy has long provided an example as the classic emigrating country where Italian born citizens were trained to seek their living for much of their lifetimes outside their own country. This theme prevailed in Italy through the nineteenth century and most of the twentieth. In fact, it is only recently that the exodus has been reversed. By the end of the 1860s, 100,000 emigrants a year were quitting the Italian homeland. This mid-century exodus found most going to Europe and South America, a phenomenon accompanied by large-scale return emigration. This pattern was to perdure in the 1880s and 1890s as mass Italian emigration turned increasingly to the United States as a major outlet. Most Italian immigrants to the United States until the last decade of the century were from northern Italy, who, although similarly plagued by the problems described, nevertheless, experienced less dislocation than emigrants from the south. Economics, although constituting a major expulsive factor was not the exclusive cause of emigration from this area. Thus, motivations ranged from a combination of social and religious transitions, personal adventure and curiosity, to efforts to avoid military service.

By comparison to their northern fellow countrymen, southern Italians were distinctly more disadvantaged, benefiting little from industrial and educational developments in Italy. Also, as a result of the lack of the amenities of life in the smaller towns of the south, fewer Italian officials desired to be stationed there. Consequently, after being assigned to these localities, upon gaining experience even these predictably less competent officials were promoted and moved to assignments in the north. Thus, the south did not have the benefit of a sustained and enlightened administrative leadership. These conditions fostered the idea that the south was lazy and incompetent — a reputation widely believed abroad. Another feature of the southern heritage was *campanilismo,* a strong sense of provincial identification which, among other things, precluded the easy adoption of community-wide institutions among Italian Americans, although the initiation of national parishes helped to overcome this background.

As the nineteenth century wore on, southern Italians became increasingly less tolerant of the landlord's yoke, looking to emigration as a solution, although the outward movement was neither a well premeditated nor systemized process. By contrast northerners brought more careful calculations into play.

At first Italian officials paid little attention to the emigration phenomenon and no government efforts were made to regulate the steamship companies and the emigration agencies which exploited the immigrants. In truth the authorities were glad to be rid of the excess population. Unsystematized as the movement may have been, the old rural institutions finally proved resilient enough to bring a measure of order into the process of emigration. Thus, it was the peasant background of skepticism and self-reliance which best served the emigrating *contadini.* In 1901 the Emigration Law passed by the Italian Parliament marked an effort to limit the activities of the steamship companies and introduce measures for safety and hygiene.

The demographics of emigration have indicated that the early period of mass emigration was a predominantly male movement. The typical pattern was for the oldest son or father to undertake a voyage to America and "try his luck". If he met with some success he would accumulate enough funds to call over the members of his family. This might take years and require improvised provisions for room and board in the interim. Many immigrants, moreover, returned to Italy to visit their families, marry, and then return to the United States.

Whereas Italian immigrant settlement patterns in the United States were rather widespread in the pre-mass immigration period, the urban northeast became the focus of concentration once the large movements began. So pronounced was this flow, it has survived to the present.

Topics covered by the interviewees range from the personal and anecdotal to discussions of public issues and well-known figures. While acknowledging that this is not an historical work in the traditional sense, topics discussed comport with extant historical records. Substantiation of important matters of politics and journalism has in fact been undertaken and should serve to provide assurance as to the accuracy of the contents.

In a studied effort to retain spontaneity, freshness and originality, the accounts recorded in this volume remain, for the most part, accurate reproductions as related to me by the interviewees. In the majority of instances the life stories described were taped by me, while in a few cases (Pieracci, Zappulla, Pinna, Grillo) the respondents preferred to write their own accounts allowing me to utilize them in the manner I deemed most helpful. In these latter situations there was a minimum of editing, while in the taped reminiscences more re-shaping and re-structuring on the part of the editor was required. Accordingly, some accounts will seem to be more spontaneous while others demonstrate a premeditated approach more akin to the preparation and forethought involved in a written style. To minimize redundancy and repetition and to increase clarity, some editing was rendered necessary in all the accounts. On the occasions wherein I did exercise my editorial prerogative, I made every effort not to intrude an "alien" style or otherwise to violate the integrity of the stories. At times this resulted in a deliberate retention of some words or expressions in Italian which are erroneous from a purist viewpoint, but which may be accepted as dialect usage — which was, in fact, quite evident among the respondents.

I trust I have kept faithful to my intention and have, therefore, served the autobiographical accounts well. To the extent that this intention was not matched by the performance, I ask the apologies of the individuals whose accounts were involved. Above all I hope and trust that I have remained faithful to the confidence placed in me by a remarkable number of Americans of Italian ancestry.

I am indebted to many people who were instrumental in the development and production of this work. First, I should like to thank the respondents whose stories are included in this volume as well as those not included who were so generous with their time. Second, I should like to thank the many friends who suggested interviewees. I also want to acknowledge the sabbatical leave granted by Nassau Community College which permitted me to undertake this research. Finally, I want to pay special tribute to the administration and staff of the Center for Migration Studies: Fr. Lydio F. Tomasi and Maggie Sullivan for their encouragement and cooperation; especially Fr. Sylvano Tomasi with whom I shared ideas concerning the theme of this book and who directed me to some of the most fruitful subjects in it.

~ONE~
The Miners

Introduction

Although conditions have improved considerably in recent years, mine work in the nineteenth and well into the twentieth centuries was notoriously harsh. The hours normally encompassed the daylight hours, Monday through Saturday. During the work week the miner spent most of his waking hours underground. His clothes were soiled and the dangers he confronted were both ubiquitous and unceasing. "We get old quickly", noted one immigrant miner. "Powder, smoke, after-damp and bad air, all combine to bring furrows to our faces and asthma to our lungs". Moreover, wages were minimal and the miner was usually required to purchase his goods from the company store which frequently overpriced its items.

Into this environment came many Italian migrants.

The personal accounts which follow include the stories of two Italian immigrant miners and the story of a woman whose father earned his livelihood through mining — an occupation she grew up with and came to know and describe both intimately and powerfully.

Saverio Rizzo is an unusual man. I first met him after he contacted me, informing me of his writings. Subsequently, I had many meetings with him and came to know him as a humble, eighty-seven year old Italian American who had emigrated in 1903 during the peak of Italian immigration to the United States. His formal education was limited to la terza, that is, three years of elementary education in nineteenth century Italy. As a teenager he came to this country to work and to live and, in the course of his active working years, he held a number of skilled and unskilled positions, many of which were in the mining industry.

Rizzo also possesses a passion for writing prose and poetry. Having written first in his native language, at the age of seventy-two he began to write in in English. Now, approaching his ninetieth year, writing continues to be his major daily work. Most of his literary works, which include, novels, essays and poetry, remain unpublished except for a few items which were published in Italian American newspapers long since extinct. For this text his writing contains much of the roughness and primitiveness of the untrained writer. Yet, these vignettes both lucidly and graphically document the intersection of Italian immigration with American society.

John Chessa's journey to the United States did not follow the usual immigration pattern via Ellis Island. His first experience in the New World was part of the historic, perhaps romantic odyssey of the Panama Canal. Chessa labored in the "big ditch" from 1910 until its completion in 1914. It was against that background that he entered his adopted land and ventured into the coal mines of western Pennsylvania. Still carrying the sicknesses of a life-time exposure to coal dust and after-damp, Chessa remains, at the age of eighty-seven, a resilient man whose impressive frame is only an indication of what must have been a sinewy strength and relentless stamina.

Chessa's story holds another interesting facet. There are few writings regarding the people from the Italian island of Sardinia who came to America. To that extent, the Chessa autobiography offers an opportunity to review the role of the Sardinian immigrants in the peopling of America.

Bruna Pieracci is one of two individuals included in this anthology whom I was unable to meet personally. In a poignant history, she carefully relates her story and that of her father, an Italian immigrant miner in the American midwest. Not following the familiar Mulberry Street path, so typical of many Italians who made their way into American life, the Pieraccis moved to the unlikely location of Iowa and dwelled there as the father worked in the mines. Because of her closeness to her father, and because of her role in the household during her mother's illness, Bruna Pieracci came to know well the physical problems confronted by the miners. In a moving and profound description she articulates the psychological stress faced by the immigrants and visited upon her own family. It is a telling story which pays tribute to the commitment and strength of character reflective of the Italian American woman.

Saverio Rizzo

I was born in the town of Cimigliano, in the province of Catanzaro, Italy, which I left at the age of sixteen in 1903. I was preceded to America by two of my brothers, one of whom was killed in a mining accident in New Jersey.

Most of the men who had emigrated from my town had intended to return, expecting to remain in America for perhaps five or six years simply to earn money. Cimigliano, however, had no industries and there was a scarcity of work and a certain amount of poverty. Yet, after a short time, some did return.

One of those who returned was a neighbor of ours who arrived from America with a few hundred dollars, which in those days was considered a great sum, and asked me if I wanted to emigrate with him on his return trip. I answered that I would be glad to come but that he would have to ask my parents' permission. He did and, since he was a good man, they did not object. He promised that he would look after me like a father, and since I was a minor and had to have a guardian, he would take on the responsibility.

It was 12:00 p.m. when my guardian and I left my home town. The railroad station was eight miles away and, since there was no means of transportation, we had to walk to meet the train at 6:00 a.m. which took us to Naples where the ship was anchored. Although it rained all the way from Cimigliano to Naples and we were saturated from head to foot, we arrived at the station in time to depart.

We boarded a third class coach which was neither comfortable nor expensive. It had "rustic" benches and no sanitary conveniences. After six hours we were in Naples where an agent of the ship company was waiting and took us to a clean hotel which served good food. Because the ship was taking on merchandise we had to wait two days before departure. When we left it was dark and we could see the flames of Vesuvius.

After nineteen days of partly rough seas in an insect laden and decrepit Spanish merchant ship, we sighted the Statue of Liberty and the New York City skyscrapers. We landed at Ellis Island where we had to pass medical examinations, which everyone dreaded since many immigrants were rejected and were returned to their native land. It was not until many years later that a law was enacted which required the immigrants to be examined at the ports of embarkation. From the ferry boat I looked at the magnitude of New York buildings and the extensive harbor and everything seemed gorgeous to me. We had no chance to visit, however, as we rushed to Grand Central Station to proceed to our destination. At Albany we changed trains and after four more hours we arrived at a small station with a few small houses around it.

"To the mine", ordered my guardian to the man with the carriage alongside the station. We jumped in and, as we sat inside, he snapped the whip and put the horse at a trot. To the mine? I asked myself, it must be the village name. The carriage came to a stop between two shanties and we descended. My guardian gave the coachman a dollar and, as he left, we entered a worn, semi-dark room, used as a food and liquor store for the miners.

This was my introduction to the mining town of Talcumville. The town I had imagined to be a beautiful place caused my heart to shrink with disappointment. My home was a dirty shanty in the camp. I thought destiny had transported me to the wrong place, but I decided to adapt myself to the circumstances of the present and hope for a better future.

I was soon introduced to the man who ran the store and who wished to be called "Uncle Gabriel". Before long I concluded that this man was not sincere in his dealings with the miners. Since it was my first day, however, I was not in a position to express my opinion. My thoughts were turned more to the conditions of that squalid location and the crowded shanty which was to become my home.

After an improvised lunch, Uncle Gabriel counseled Tommaso and me to take a nap on his bed in his room behind the store. Tommaso, who drank most of the wine and was feeling its effect accepted the offer. I declined with the excuse that I wanted to see the men as they came home. Basically, however, I only wanted to be alone to meditate on my present situation, and to try to face the future with more confidence.

Six p.m. was quitting time. From the direction of the mine, half a mile away, I saw the miners trudging along a dirty pathway toward the shanties. As they advanced, I noticed they resembled snowmen, with the pure white of the talcum dust. There were twenty-five miners, one holster, a blacksmith, and ten men to take care of the mill where the material was pulverized and converted to powder. Two teamsters hauled the material to the mill. With the exception of the teamsters, the men had all been recruited by Uncle Gabriel, and he seemed to have some kind of control over them. He had obtained the concession for a store on company property where the miners were required to buy all their commodities as a recompense to him for having found work for them. No one was permitted to trade in the village stores where the prices were lower and the merchandise of better quality. Any transgression would have cost the transgressor the loss of his job.

Talcumville, a cluster of white painted houses, was half a mile away, but the miners rarely visited there. They worked during the weekdays, and on Sunday they spent the time playing cards for beverages from which Uncle Gabriel harvested double profit.

Tommaso joined me then and, when the men came close, they all rushed to welcome him.

"Who's the new miner?" asked one of the men.

"He's my nephew", said Tommaso, "and he ain't going to be a miner".

"Of course not. He's too young, and too gentle to be one", said a few miners in unison.

"I will take care of him", interposed Uncle Gabriel who had joined the group.

"Many thanks, Uncle Gabriel", I said.

"And now, all you men hurry and wash up. We must have a little party in honor of the newly arrived", he suggested.

The party meant selling more beer and more profit to him. The men went inside to change their working clothes. That done, they came out, filled a fifteen foot long vessel with water, and washed themselves. The water had been pulled with a pail from an abandoned mine where the drinking water was also obtained. I observed that the water was polluted, but decided not to reveal it to the men. I did not want to alarm them and start something that would have angered Uncle Gabriel. There were no women, so the men prepared their own meals. Since not all liked the same food, they had divided themselves in groups in accordance with culinary taste. They started the fire between two cement blocks on top of which they placed their cooking utensils. They ate at one long table with a bench on either side.

That evening Uncle Gabriel, Tommaso and I joined them. Uncle Gabriel made sure the table was well stocked with beer and he suggested that I assimilate myself to the custom and the food. "Give me a little time, and I will", I said, "I learn fast", I added. "Good", he said, "and as a start, tomorrow morning you will learn to be a blacksmith's helper".

"That's wonderful!" said a few miners in unison before I had the chance to thank him.

"Yes", said Uncle Gabriel. "And while he learns, he will earn three dollars per week", he added with simulated benevolence.

"It's not an auspicious start", observed Tommaso, "and three dollars per week is no money".

"He may get a raise as he begins to learn", said Uncle Gabriel. To me, three dollars a week seemed a fortune. Converted to Italian money, I was going to earn triple the amount my father was earning at home. What I did not know was that there was also triple the cost of living.

I was also unaware of a fraudulent collusion between Uncle Gabriel and the superintendent of the mine to deduct one dollar a week out of the miners' wages for the "privilege" of living in a shanty. Since I was classified as an apprentice and a worker out of the mine, my deduction was two dollars out of my regular five dollar wage.

Because the superintendent manipulated the payroll, the company was not aware of the cheating.

Fearing the loss of their jobs, the men did not dare protest the abusive treatment, and the usurpers divided the loot without fear of discovery.

I was unaware of the two dollar deduction since Uncle Gabriel had set my wage, and it was not marked on my pay envelope.

There were no diversionary activities, so the men spent their free time playing card games for beer making more profit for Uncle Gabriel. He had a few who promoted the games and received special treatment and often free drinks in return. Such vile Judases can be found among any agglomeration of men whose only desire is to profit regardless of the harm they inflict.

Most of the men were penniless at the end of the week and some were in debt. Only a few, like Tommaso, saved a small portion of their earnings to help support their family in Italy. Uncle Gabriel was not happy about this, but refrained from showing his displeasure. Tommaso knew all of Uncle Gabriel's tricks, but he too kept his job by remaining silent. So, what I have described I learned weeks after our arrival.

Tommaso and I had gone to work the next morning after our arrival. He resumed his old job as drill runner, which paid ten dollars per week and I as a blacksmith's helper which, without the deduction, was worth five dollars per week.

My first duty was to kindle the fire, which was a simple action and required little physical energy. The place was dusty and, as it was still warm, it was not very pleasant. Communication with the blacksmith resembled that of deaf-mutes. By quitting time, however, I had learned that *il martello* was called hammer; the *incudine,* anvil; the *tenaglia,* tongs; and the *mantice,* blower. "It wasn't too bad for one day", I mused, as I walked toward the shanty where the men asked me if I liked the job.

I told them that in time I might be a good blacksmith myself. Of course, I did not really want to be one since I considered it too rough and somewhat hard.

There was no party that evening, but the men gathered in groups to play cards and drink beer. Uncle Gabriel asked me if I would like to earn an extra dollar per week by taking care of his books and I accepted. After all, I figured, that dollar was equivalent to five *lire,* which I could send to my parents.

I helped Uncle Gabriel all evening and on Sundays, so it would not interfere with my regular job. On Fridays I added up the miners' debts to be ready for collection on Saturday which was payday. Uncle Gabriel was semiliterate, and Tommaso had helped him before. Tommaso had found many alterations in the books which he had not revealed. Now, he revealed these to me, warning me to keep it a secret. I did not want to be an accomplice, but I needed that extra dollar and decided not to expose the systematic fraud. Thus, I became the helper of the two men, one an experienced mechanic and the other an unscrupulous thief.

Tommaso joined the men in the preparation of the evening supper and, for the second time, we ate our meal which had been placed on top of the long table with no tablecloth.

At bedtime I went to sleep in the bunk which had been assigned to me.

The room had two lines of bunks to accomodate twenty-five miners. The bunks had no springs and the mattresses were filled with straw.

It was not comfortable sleeping on such bunks, but I had to get used to it. In fact, the environment of the entire place was not as encouraging as I had expected, but I did not show my disappointment.

As he had promised my parents, Tommaso did everything possible to keep me happy. Since he could not have guessed what was going on in my mind, he had the impression that I was satisfied. I missed my parents' love and the friendliness of all my young companions, but I did not lose hope in a better future. After all, Talcumville was not the entire United States, and I was not chained to Talcumville. Tommaso had already hinted that as soon as he found a better place we would move away, so I endured the discomfort.

Winter came and with it snow, sub-zero temperature and gloom. I did not feel the rigor of winter at the shop, but going and coming I had to trample on three to four feet of snow and, at the shanty, the freezing North wind shrilled its fury through the cracked walls. The potbelly stove emitted scanty heat and the smell of the bituminous coal made breathing difficult. Sometimes, during the nights, I had to get up to inhale a little fresh air by putting my mouth in one of the wall's cracks. I felt so miserable that I wanted to run away from the place, but where could I go. I was in a strange land, I could not yet speak the language and it was winter time. So, I endured the inevitable, until spring would displace winter. Everything was against me there except hope in the future, and that was my only encouragement.

No matter how low the temperature was, or how deep the snow, I continued to go to work, and I was admired for my endurance.

Within six months of our arrival, the mine suspended operation for lack of orders and all the miners left to find work elsewhere. Luckily, Tommaso, who was still my guardian, knew another mining town called Witherbee, New York, two hundred miles to the Northeast where iron ore was mined.

Before looking for work there we found a boarding house that was clean. The food was well prepared and tasteful and reminded me of my mother's cooking. The price was three dollars per week for lodging and food, but was a paradise in comparison to the filthy shanty of Talcumville.

Having established our residence, we went to the company employment office to ask for work. My guardian was hired immediately but since I was too young, the clerk hesitated to hire me. So my guardian warned him that if he refused me a job, he would refuse his.

Since there was a scarcity of men, the clerk changed his mind and hired me. The miner's wage at that time was a dollar and a half a day, but mine would be one dollar a day for working five ten hour days and eight hours on Saturday.

Since my pay was double that of Talcumville it raised my hopes for the future. The only thing I missed was reading books and newspapers but I soon subscribed to *Il Progresso Italo-Americano,* which was published in New York.

It was the first time an Italian newspaper had reached that mine town and I used to read it and pass the news to the other miners who, in the majority, were illiterate. I began to give reading lessons to those who wished to learn, without asking compensation, thinking it was a social duty to help those who needed it. To my disappointment, however, only three young men took advantage of my offer.

The man in Witherbee who had obtained a concession similar to that of "Uncle Gabriel" was using the same method, but in a more lenient way, because the majority of the men there came from the same region of southern Italy. He collected one dollar per month from the men and warned them not to buy any commodities in other stores or bars if they wanted to be able to get credit in case of a depression. He had an agent on Mulberry Street in New York who recruited incoming immigrants for the mines. It was for this service that he had obtained the concession from the two companies that owned the mine, Witherbee-Sherman, and Port Henry Iron Ore Co.

One day I met a newcomer and befriended him. He was kind and seemed more a philosopher than a laborer. Here I found an intelligent man with whom I could converse in fluent Italian. He disliked all those who cursed, and pitied all those who prayed, considering cursing an exasperation of ignorance and praying the hope of the weak.

Since there existed no safety rules at the time, the danger of an accidental death was ever present. After ten deaths in one year had been ignored by the company, my new friend decided to quit the job and the village to look for work elsewhere. He counseled me to go with him, and since I admired the man I took his advice, but at the same time I hated to disassociate myself from the man who had guided me as a father. Observing my hesitance, however, Tommaso also resolved to quit the dangerous place.

My friend had spent some time in New York City and selected it as our new residence. One of my "pupils" who had a widowed sister in New York also left to reunite himself with her. Once in New York we had no difficulty finding work. Tommaso found work in subway construction; my new friend who had some accounting experience, was employed in one of the many improvised immigrants' banks; and Giuseppe (my "pupil") and I found jobs in a factory which manufactured paper containers for the Colgate Soap Company of Jersey City, New Jersey. Here I earned five and a half dollars per week. When we were hired we were not told that our daily working time was dependent on orders received. That is, we had to report to the factory every morning, but if there were no work to be done we still had to wait for a possible order and get paid only for the time we had worked on it. It was an arbitrary and abusive position. I remember one week in which I earned only seventy five cents.

Now, it was not my ambition to become a millionaire in this land of equal opportunity, but with the wages I was getting I could not even have gathered a little fortune.

Equality is a euphemistic word, and, I think, it is used to justify inequality. A young man who has the chance to go to college can not be classified equal to one who has not the same opportunity. The same can be said in comparing a boy who inherits a fortune and one who inherits poverty at his birth.

Now, I do not note this reflection from envy, but only to expose the inconsistency of "equal opportunity". Another falsehood is the assumed justification of those who receive inheritance that their ancestors worked hard to accumulate their riches. The historical facts are that the riches were, and are, gathered through the exploitation of their workers, and the fraudulent acquisition of natural resources. My parents worked all their lives and although they tried to save a little out of their meager earnings, they could not succeed in keeping me in school, or at home. Their only contribution to my future was the fare which brought me to a foreign land, in search of work and the possibility for a better future. It was here that I heard that anyone can become a millionaire. Of course I did not believe in such nonsense, and my first three jobs proved that I was right.

Yet, I stuck to my job at Colgate because there was a chance to learn the intricate machine which had been assigned to me and to be put on piece work which meant 17 cents per thousand containers on which I fastened a tin top.

I had to use both hands, and one foot. I had to pick up the empty paper shell (container) with my left hand from the bin, pass it to the right hand, put the tin on top, and then place it on the pivot which I lifted with my foot to the spinning wheel which fastened the top to the shell. This was a difficult and dangerous operation. Any false movement and the spinning tin would cut my index finger.

It took me a few months to reach the speed of one thousand an hour, which meant from eight to ten dollars per week, depending on the orders received from the Colgate Company.

The factory was located near Washington Market, thirteen blocks from where I was living and to save the ten cents a day carfare, I walked there and back.

The flat I lived in had four rooms on the third floor of the building where there were two windows facing the street, and two windows in the back room, which was the kitchen. The two center rooms had no windows. There was a toilet between two flats which was used by two families (twelve persons).

There were five women (two of whom were sisters, and one a widow), two men, and a three year old boy who was the son of the widow. The widow's husband had died a short time before the child's birth, and she had taken an oath not to remarry, dedicating her future to her son.

As the head of the household, the widow acted more like a mother than a housekeeper. She paid fourteen dollars a month rent, while we each paid three dollars. This gave her four dollars a month profit from which she paid the gas used for lighting and cooking. The women cooked the meals when they returned from work and we all ate together, dividing the cost of the food at the end of the week.

Because we all were confronted with the same problems, there existed an atmosphere of sincere friendship. To illustrate the sincere cordiality which reigned in that house, I recall that the women, to add a little more to the meager wages they earned, used to carry home bundles of apparel to work on at home during the evenings. They had to do this work in the kitchen where the three men slept. We would unfold the bed, undress and lie down to sleep, as the women were absorbed in their work. Many times they would work past midnight, rise again at half past five in the morning to prepare breakfast and get ready to walk with the bundles they had worked on the night before to the factory eight blocks away. Their work hours were from seven in the morning to five thirty at night with half an hour for lunch. There was no union where they worked so they had to endure the abuses of the sweatshop.

Frequently, while the women sewed at night I would narrate novels such as Carolina Invernisio's *Il figlio di nessuno, La sepolta viva, Il figlio dell'anarchico,* and *Genoveffa, La Promessa Sposa,* and operas "Lucia di Lammermoor", "Madame Butterfly", "La Tosca", "La Bohéme", "Il Trovatore", and "L'Aida". They liked to listen to my narration, but as all the stories were based on tragic themes there would be tears in their eyes as I read.

I continued to work until I was notified that, due to the lack of orders, some men had to be laid off and, since I was one of the last hired, I was the first.

The foreman had promised that he would send for us as soon as they received some orders, but I started to look for work the next day and continued to search for many days. The widow's brother had also been fired, so we both visited the same places. Some places simply had signs posted, "No help wanted today". Having visited the industrial section we reached Washington Park, flanked by New York University on the east side and luxurious buildings on the north side. Looking west and south there stood the slum; a contrasting and disconcerting vista.

Near there I looked and I saw the sign for Thompson Street, and another to Mulberry Street which reminded my friend that Mulberry Street would take us to the "Ritrovo dei Paisani" which was also the Gilberti Hotel.

There, we found a three story building owned by Vitaliano Gilberti. The street floor consisted of a bar and dining room, which had a small room which was partitioned for use as a bank and office for receiving and helping migrants. It was presided over by a man named Don Michele, who obtained the lists of the incoming immigrants from the navigation companies and met the new arrivals at the piers. It was in this office where Uncle Gabriel and Giuseppe Scozzafava from Witherbee recruited men who needed a job.

In the back was a small kitchen where Don Michele's wife, who was called "Zia Maria" by all those who knew her, cooked a delicious preparation called *u spezziatiello* which was a mixture of veal, liver, lungs, fresh tomatoes and hot peppers, which she sold for 25 cents, bread included.

The first and second floors were used as a hotel for the incoming and outgoing immigrants and transient co-nationals.

When we arrived, we ordered two portions of the *spezziatiello* and two beers, and because we had not eaten since we had left the house, we devoured it. It was a delicious dinner for a moderate price (30 cents).

As we were about to leave, a group of men arrived. Mr. Gilberti rushed to receive them. "Signor Scozzafava!" he exclaimed as he extended his hand to the men. I looked and there was the man from Witherbee whom I suspected of being my distant cousin. Now, I had the chance to find out, I thought. I approached him and I asked him from what region of Italy he had come. He remembered having seen me at Witherbee, so he extended his hand to me and asked, "Why you want to know?"

"Because my mother's maiden name is Maria Scozzafava", I said.
"And your father Tommaso Rizzo?" he added.
"Yes", I said.
"Second, or third cousins", he replied and took me in his arms. I was so delighted by such an unexpected discovery that I forgot my present predicament. I had a cousin now, and an agent of a big iron ore company, who would put me to work.

He relinquished his embrace, and stared at me with a smile. Having left the town before my birth he was unaware of my existence.

"Why have your parents let you come to America so young?" he asked, "And how long have you been here?"

"I will explain everything later on. Now, I want you to know that I am happy to meet you, and I hope you will help me to find a job."

We returned to Witherbee with my cousin where we went to work in the mines for 10 hours a day and 9 on Saturdays; the pay was $1.50 per day. My cousin selected a house for me to board in, which was inhabited by a family from my home town, so I was pleased. All the families who rented company houses were obligated, under fear of eviction, to take in boarders. There were a few private proprietors of small tracts of land, but virtually no private houses for rent. In addition to Italians there were Hungarians and Polish miners and, although there was some antipathy among the three groups, there was rarely a physical encounter. This was not so with the first groups who had been brought there. They had encountered the hostility of the Anglo-Saxons. It was the courage of a group of Italians (my cousin included) who, by fighting against them, demolished their arrogance. This was not an easy task. They had to take turns at night with rifles in hand to defend themselves and their houses, from being dynamited during the night. In fact, five sticks of dynamite were found under the store one morning. It had been a miracle they said, because the fuse which had been attached to the dynamite was defective. I met two old men who had participated in the vigilance. They had left the place and returned after many years to establish a permanent residence there.

Mining is a dangerous position, but many accidents can be avoided by using precautionary means. The superintendent of the mine where I was working was an exacting man when it came to production but he saw to it that the safety of the men came first. He directed the mine's operation at the mine and not from the office. He did not want to be responsible for any loss of life or injuries. Destiny, however, is cruel and capricious.

One morning his assistant saw a crack in the side of a column above where the men were working and he reported it to the superintendent. Both went and got a thirty foot ladder to find out how dangerous the crack was. The superintendent decided to examine it himself, and as he hit the rock with a hammer, a chunk of ore fell on top of him and his assistant who was holding the ladder, crushing both under its impact. Their bodies were recovered in pieces and placed in wooden boxes, because there was no possibility to reconstruct them.

There had been other tragedies, but that one was the most frightful.

Joe, my friend, returned to New York, but I decided to stay a little longer. The mine suspended operations for one week as a mourning period for the men. When it was reopened I started to work in my new job which paid more and was less hazardous.

Now, it was the dead superintendent's oldest son who, having been elevated to his father's position was directing the operation of the mine. He, however, did not go down into the mines, but left it to the foreman to direct the men.

Eventually, I returned to New York City. One day I was walking along Delancey Street where the subway connecting the Williamsburg Bridge was under construction. It was quitting time, and I saw a gang of laborers coming out from the underground. I saw a neatly dressed man with only one arm. Evidently, he was the foreman. I stopped him asking if he could hire me.

"We're doing a polishing job", he said. "That is concrete finishing. If you think that you can do this kind of work, you can start in the morning."

The job paid a dollar and a half per day and eight hours per day. That meant three dollars more and two hours less work a day for me. The foreman was very kind and gave me the needed instructions; the work did not require much experience, so I had no difficulty performing it. I had to be careful to keep this job and, to be more secure, I started to bring a box of small cigars to the foreman every Monday morning, which he appreciated, not as a bribe, but as a gentle gift from me. He used to call me "kid" and treated me as such.

We had reached Canal Street and the junction of the B.M.T. and I.R.T. subways when one morning a young man started to yell insulting and obscene words at us, followed by a volley of stones and broken pieces of concrete. He was the son of the contractor who had just come from a party, and he charged that the work we were doing was not necessary.

He fired the entire gang, including the foreman.

This time I did not feel discouraged. Having worked steadily for eight months I had saved enough money to keep me going without a job for some time. Still, I did not take advantage of this and I started to look for work the same day.

Finally, I decided to return to the upstate mining and found that everything had changed during my absence. Even the people looked happier and somewhat better off economically. The two companies had built a washroom outside the mines where the men could wash themselves before going home. They had also built a big rooming house, which was run by my cousin, for those who wanted to live separated from the families. There was a cook to prepare the meals for them for only twelve dollars per month.

The town had begun to resemble the town I had come from in Italy and the majority of the workers came from two villages called Cimigliano and Arena or, Calabria.

Counting the workers and their families there were more than three hundred.

Their industriousness made the town a pleasant place to live. What the Anglo-Saxons had not been able to do in a hundred years or more, the Italians had accomplished since immigrating. Most of the families made their wine, and raised pigs, chickens, and a few cows. There existed no more antipathies among Italians, Polish and Hungarians, since the latter groups had learned much from the Italians.

Only one Italian contaminated the town by extorting a tribute from the miners. He paid for it with twenty years in jail. He had tried to organize a "mafia-type" society, but only five joined him and they too landed in jail. An investigator found that this man had two thousand dollars in the bank after having worked only a few months. Following the disappearance of a young man of his society who had testified against him, the extortionist was arrested and received a severe penalty (20 years). The suspicion was that the young man had been murdered.

The Anglo-Saxons had their own labor society which they arbitrarily called the American Federation of Labor. I say arbitrarily because they used it more as a private club than a labor union. I called it to the attention of a few of my friends and decided to ask the president of the society if we could join them. We were accepted and gradually most of the Italians became members, followed by the Hungarians and the Poles, so we became a multi-nationalities federation.

What we needed, to become a labor union, now was a charter from the national union. One week after writing for it, a delegate was sent from the national office in Albany to act as organizer. He was accompanied by a young Polish student who had been expelled from the Warsaw College because of his liberal ideology. Accordingly, he sought refuge in this country.

The delegate's name was O'Connor and he was an intelligent man. To avoid unnecessary disturbance he rented a room at a hotel outside the companies' territory and asked for a few of our people to help in the organizing work. I was selected as one and went to meet him. After asking a few significant questions and being given the right answers, he accepted me.

I worked among the Italians, and the Polish young man among the Polish workers as Mr. O'Connor gave us the necessary instructions. Since both companies were hostile to unionism we had to do our proselytizing in secret and avoid being trapped in any discussions with the companies' thugs. Lacking the legal authority to stop us from organizing the men, the companies used other means to obstruct us. For example, the Town Hall, a picturesque stone building which had been built by the companies on their land, could not be used for meetings or other social affairs without the companies' permission. Having found out about our work we were notified that we could not use the hall for any of our meetings.

A barkeeper of Mineville, a town a mile away, offered us a large room behind the bar, and we started to meet there. Having received the charter and having a meeting place out of the companies' grounds we came out in the open.

Two weeks later a general meeting was called and after discussing many topics, two of my friends arose and proposed my nomination for Vice-President of the Italian group.

Seconded by the delegate, I was elected by acclamation.

I made a speech which lasted fifteen minutes and I remember my closing peroration: "The companies are strong by controlling the territory which surrounds us, and they also can evict us out of their houses, but Witherbee is not America and they cannot stop us from getting out of this enclosed camp. "

"We can travel freely in this blessed land and enjoy its beauties. They have the economic power, but we have the physical power which they need more than we need theirs. This enclosed territory will not produce any profit without our physical power. So let us stick together and demand our deserved rights. Our first demand is the eight hour workday, which needs no debate. We will discuss other rights later on."

Beside the eight hour workday we demanded that the dollar a month collection go to the women who were doing the cooking and the washing for the men instead of to the "bordant" (my cousin) and we demanded the hiring of the men at the companies' offices and the liberty to buy our necessities at other stores. The Polish student was elected Vice-President of the Polish and Hungarian members. The President was an Anglo-Saxon.

As Vice-Presidents we received 17 dollars per week from the national office at Albany.

We won all the demands except the eight hour workday, which we considered more important and were more entitled to, because there was a federal law which called for it for all who worked in the mines. We notified the companies of our intention to strike, without result. So, we declared the strike, an action which was approved by the entire membership.

When we got up in the morning to start our picketing we were confronted by twenty-five thugs armed with long clubs and a few with guns. Management had collected them during the night inside the saloons of the nearby villages — a bunch of bums to whom honest work was an anomaly. In looking around we saw only big signs with the inscription "Private Property, No Trespassing" so we had only the main roads on which to walk and a small square near the Post Office to assemble. There were two company policemen, one riding a horse and the other afoot, following us in each step, and often trying to start an argument.

The town of Port Henry, three miles away, fortunately had sent a marshall to watch for any transgressions by the thugs, and his presence avoided many fights.

The same day, all those who lived in the company houses received notices to vacate the houses within thirty days if they did not go back to work. I also received notice, but I was given only three days, meaning that I was considered more dangerous. I showed the note to the delegate and he told me that I had thirty days more to add to the three.

For me it was not bad news, I could have left the same day, but for the head of a family the announcement was a discouraging problem, so many resolved to go back to their jobs. Some who had come recently and had no money to travel and look for work elsewhere also decided to resume work as did the ones whose families in the old country waited for the usual money order at the end of the month. In all, however, only a few refused to give up the fight.

I, as Vice-President, refused to be intimidated and, although I was followed continuously by the policeman on horseback, I remained there another two weeks. During this period I shared a room with the delegate and the student.

We had won all of our terms and to have a little discomfort is a reward. I only regretted the persistent surveillance of that policeman. He really was an arrogant servant of the companies. When finally I decided to leave he even followed me to the steps of the train. The delegate and the student left a few days later. The three of us knew that we had planted the seed of the union which would germinate better results in the future.

One week later I also left New York, and decided to go to Winooski, Vermont, where the American Woolen Company had a big factory in which a few hundred Italians of both sexes were working. There were eleven Italian families, two of which had left Witherbee at the time of the strike, so when I arrived I found board with one of them. I got a clean room and the cooking was well prepared and tasteful. There was a big Italian store where Italian imported delicacies could be bought. There was also an Italian bakery where bread and Italian style pastry was baked and distributed daily for miles around and even across the Champlain River as far as Plattsburgh, Ticonderoga, and Witherbee.

An Italian farmer three miles from the village had his two sons visit the same localities every day to sell fruits, fresh vegetables and milk. At Burlington, a beautiful city across the Winooski River, there was a theater and there were many stores selling all kinds of merchandise. There existed no discord among the peoples of different nationalities, nor among the Italians.

When I arrived, the company had received an order for thousands of blankets for the Italian Army which was fighting a war in Turkey. I had no trouble getting a job. I was hired as a filling carrier, carrying the filling to the weavers. I served fifty weavers. As the order had to be rushed, the material was not coming out perfect and there were holes in many blankets. Someone reported this to the Boston Consulate who immediately sent an Italian inspector. All defective blankets were set aside and since they could not be repaired, were destroyed.

While I was tending my work I watched the weaver and within a short time I learned to weave. I asked and I was given a loom to weave blankets, which I made sure had no holes.

Weaving was an easy job, but it was not too healthful for the ears. We used to communicate by the movement of our lips. I endured the deafening noise of fifty looms running at once and kept working and earning a good wage.

Then, there was a tragedy. There was a dye room with a ten foot diameter tank to dip the material in the liquid color. An Italian attended it, and kept the liquid boiling to a certain degree so the colors would be absorbed evenly and he used a pole to push down any piece of cloth. No one knows what happened but the man fell in the tank, and according to the doctor's report, died instantly. This tragedy saddened the entire community.

There was another tragedy concerning two first cousins, one with a wife and children, the other single and living in the same house.

Early one morning the single cousin was found dead in front of the house. He had been stabbed by his cousin who suspected that he was having an affair with his wife. The man was arrested and given a twenty years to life sentence. This was a shameful blot to the entire community.

Another drama was avoided by the personal intervention of the Italian Consul. The company had a freight yard alongside the factory where coal for the boilers was received in large freight cars. Since some of the coal was being stolen the company had put two guards to patrol the entire company's property. One morning a young French Canadian was found dead under one of the cars. An Italian man and his pregnant wife were seen leaving a house nearby, as they had been seen many times before, picking pieces of coal which had fallen on the tracks. Others were doing the same, but this couple was selected as the killers and was arrested.

Everyone was convinced of their innocence except the guards and the judge who interrogated them, who did not even consider the woman's pregnancy. After the Consul's arrival they were found innocent. She gave birth at home to a boy who died at the age of 72, two years ago at Bethpage, Long Island.

The man who had been communicating with the Boston Consul had emigrated from Messina, Sicily. He had come to work in Winooski at the time of the Lawrence strike when the company was forced to transfer some of the orders to the Winooski factory. His name was Dominico Rizzo and called me cousin when he found out that my name was also Rizzo. His political tendencies were revolutionary which harmonized well with my liberal ideology. With the end of the Italian War in Turkey came a slack in work, so I decided to return to New York. Once in the city, I went to Bayonne, New Jersey, to try to get a job in one of the refineries.

During World War I, I was employed with the Texaco Oil Company in Bayonne, New Jersey which was shipping gasoline and bituminous oil to the army. I had been hired as a warehouseman and worked with two gangs of fifteen men apiece covering two shifts — night and day. It was hard work, but since we were working for a just cause we endured it. We had an Italian timekeeper who called me one day and asked me if I would like to have his job. I thought that he was kidding me but he was not. He had filed an application for policeman and had been accepted. He gave me a few hours of instruction and I became a timekeeper. In helping the checkers from time to time I learned also how to check, so I was used as such when needed.

I worked for the company for five consecutive years.

I am not a proud man, but in considering that I improved my position in almost every job I held during my lifetime I do feel proud.

In the period following World War I, I continued to earn a living for my family, but I also kept in touch with Italian events. There were a couple of incidents I recall which deeply affected the Italians in America in the 1920s and 1930s. One was the Sacco-Vanzetti tragedy which was a sad occurence for Italian communities all over the world, and at the same time a shameful blot to the American judicial system. On the evening of their execution a vigil was held in Union Square in which all my friends and I participated. The crowd not only filled the park, but also the space around it. It was a spectacle of tremendous indignation. At the north side of the park was a truck with an electric battery and a pole with a red electric bulb attached to it. No one knew why it was there, but at the moment of execution it let out a flash. A tremendous cry filled the space. There was sobbing and tears, mixed with condemnation against the judge and the Governor of Massachusetts who had refused clemency to the victims. The Italian press had put up a big fight, but to no avail. The victims' nationality and their liberal ideology worked against them. We went home and spent a sleepless night.

An event in which the entire Italian community rejoiced was the arrival of the squadron of Italian airplanes under the command of General Balbo. I was in the elevated train on my way to New York and it had reached Eastern Parkway when all the passengers rushed out of the train to look at the distant sky. I ran out and there were 10 airplanes in a *V* formation. It was a grand spectacle which, after so many years still lingers in my mind. Twenty-three Italian aviators had arrived to bring glory to Italian aviation, and our country.

The following day there was a parade on lower Broadway and a reception at City Hall where General Balbo received the keys to the city from the Mayor. The park and the surrounding spaces were crowded to capacity by Italians and admirers from other nationalities. I, and many others from Jamaica, participated in honoring our national heroes. It was a grand spectacle of admiration.

Following this happiness there was a terrible tragedy a number of years later when General Balbo crashed mysteriously and died in his native land. At the time there was a suspicion that Mussolini, frightened by the popularity of Balbo, which threatened his absolute power, had sent one of his servants to tamper with the airplane's engine.

The election of Fiorello LaGuardia was not only an honor for the Italians, but a benediction for all who loved honesty. He was a combative man and cleaned the dirty political mess which was polluting City Hall. Even today when we mention LaGuardia, he is praised as the best Mayor New York ever had.

In the 1930s I had a friend in Jamaica, Long Island, whom I visited and who told me to look for work at the Jamaica Water Supply Company. The foreman there was an Italian and I had no trouble being hired as a ditch digger. The job paid five dollars for working ten hours a day. After I had handled only pencils and pens for five years with the Texas Oil Company it was no pleasure to handle a pick and shovel now. Yet, I needed a job and I had to endure that kind of work. We had a young engineer's helper who sometimes substituted for the foreman and who, after noticing the bleeding blisters in my hands, transferred me to a gardener's helper. That was a more amenable work for me. With the Second World War, I was offered a position as a patrol man. It was my job then to patrol the pump houses, read and register the pressure, and stop and start them according to the pressure. After that I was promoted to filter engineer. We had no union and I passed the word to organize ourselves. The president of the company was against it, but it was not like Witherbee and we did not encounter many difficulties. Having a union, we demanded a reasonable raise and better working conditions. As with all companies, the Jamaica Water and Supply Company refused to concede to the workers demands so we had a short strike — short, because our demands were justified.

After twenty-seven years of steady work for this company at good pay and, finally, having reached the 65 year age limit demanded by law, I had to retire.

I could have continued to work, but since my working hours were from 12:00 p.m. to 8:00 a.m., I thought it was not healthful to work in so many different localities and different kinds of work without extensive interruptions. Now, I think I am entitled to some rest. So, as I become physically idle, my mind remains alert. To keep it occupied I decided to write a novel in English. Having finished one I started another, and another. Now, at the age of eighty-seven I have six completed manuscripts which I wish to have published. Will I get my wish? I doubt it, but I don't give up trying.

John D. Chessa

My name is John Chessa, pronounced "Cesa" in Italian, and a common name among the Sardinians. I was born in a Sardinian town called Pattada in the year 1891. Now I am 88 years old and still strong despite the black lung disease I received from the coal mines. I worked in the Pennsylvania coal mines for 19 years in Windber, a town close to Johnstown. I also worked for a number of coal companies including one of the biggest coke companies in the country. In 1922 the coal mines were struck with the biggest strike in the country when over 600,000 coal miners went on strike. After spending six months on strike, I did not return to my old company but tried another. Then I went back to Italy but after some time, I once again returned to the United States. My wife did not wish for me to return to the coal mines after this, so I decided to go to Port Washington, New York where I had many friends.

Let me backtrack. When I lived in Pattada I went to school to the fifth grade which was then considered enough for most of us. To go beyond the fifth grade we would have had to leave the town and not many of us did. I left home originally to work on the Panama Canal, where I remained for fifty-two months. I started in Gatun where I remained for two years. Gatun is about 30 to 35 miles from Colon and is one of the bigger cities. In 1912 I moved to Miraflores on the Pacific Coast and I later worked on other Canal locations. The Canal was completed in 1914 at which time we were given three choices. Because the workers were Italian, French or Greek, we could go to Italy, France or Greece and the United States government would pay for the return voyages. I did not want to go back to the other side so I paid my own fare of $30.00 and, after a five day trip, arrived in New York. At that time in 1914 there was no work anywhere. However, some of my friends and my brother-in-law informed me of work in the coal mines of Pennsylvania which were operating only two or three days a week. Since I did not have any other work I decided to go into the mines. Gradually, I became used to working in the mines and did not mind it because it was piece work and I could make my own salary. The normal salary was not too bad, and things really picked up when World War I began. Then we were working day and night.

I had first wanted to go to Panama in 1908; two years before I did go in 1910. There were 136 people from Pattada, Sardinia who were recruited to work on the Canal at that time. One hundred twenty-three of them were destined to go to Panama while thirteen who did not have sufficient fare were able to get only to France. The Italian Consul in Panama at the time, had sent a telegram advising against this emigration since the host country did not recognize everyone's rights. So, *en route* to Panama in 1908 we were forced to stay for two or three days in the port of Genoa. We finally had to return to Pattada. When the opportunity came again in 1910 I went to Panama, taking the roundabout way through France. Italy did not want to cooperate with the company building the Canal since that company refused to insure the workers. Unsuccessful in obtaining workers directly from Italy, the Canal building company went to France to seek its workers. We learned about this and took the boat to France.

The American government also refused to insure the workers so that if the workers died, or broke a leg there would be no compensation for their families. The French government was inclined to go along with this arrangement because it had a background in Panama, having attempted to build the Canal there previously. A number of us from Sardinia, Greece and Spain went to France to arrange for work on the Canal. There were also a number of Sicilians and Calabrese. There were a considerable number of Calabrese in Panama City who had first arrived there about thirty years before when France originally started to build the Canal. When the venture failed these Calabrese remained there and were present when we arrived from Sardinia.

When the French company started building there, its people were hurt because of the malaria disease. Since they could not obtain sufficient numbers of white workers they began to import Chinese workers. Thousands of Chinese died from the sickness in a short time. When the United States took over the building of the Canal it instituted many more sanitary conditions and employed many people to look out for the health needs of the people with the effect that the mosquito problem was finally controlled. Then the area started to build up. By 1912 the worst of the malaria problem was over although there was still a considerable amount of the disease during the 1906—1911 period.

We had malaria in Sardinia, but not like it was in Panama. At the time there were no cures for the illness except for doses of quinine. After a quinine dosage, if you lived, you were cured.

Work on the Panama Canal brought a salary of twenty cents an hour for digging six days a week. There was overtime on occasion, for which, after ten hours a day, you were paid time and a half. My first stint there was in February 1910 and I worked for 29 straight days, including Sundays and two holidays, Lincoln's Birthday and Washington's Birthday, for which we received time and a half. Work on Sundays was also paid time and a half. The salary I earned working on the Canal was pretty good and compared favorably with what workers were getting paid in the United States at the time.

The Italian workers on the Canal generally got along well with those of other nationalities (*i.e.,* French, Spanish, etc.). There were some problems as a result of some prejudices which popped up from time to time, but overall they got along. There were no Italian newspapers available in Panama and to get along we conversed in Spanish. They spoke real Spanish there, better than in Spain itself. In 1944 I received a pension for this service. In 1944 a law was passed giving Panama Canal workers, with over three years of service, a pension. I did not find out about this law until several years later when my daughter learned about it in school. I wrote to Washington and received the necessary papers to apply for the pension. In a few weeks they sent me back-pay and a monthly pension of $17.00, which was later raised to $19.00, which pays for cigarettes.

I was at the Canal when the first boat came through Miraflores. Shortly afterwards they laid us off. At the time of the opening there were many dignitaries from Washington. Earlier, in 1910, I had seen Theodore Roosevelt in Gatun. I did not learn much English up to then since Spanish was the spoken language there. There were of course, those who spoke English and those people usually were able to obtain better jobs. I was 18 years old when I started working in Panama and 22 by the time the Canal was finished, at which time I was not yet married.

Upon coming to this country I worked for a time in the coal mines of Pennsylvania along with other workers of mixed nationalities including

Italians, Polish and Irish. I had heard a lot about the United States from people in my home town in the 1906—1908 period. At the time, our knowledge of this country was that if there was general nationwide prosperity, everybody would be working. Compared to conditions in Italy, which were very poor then, this was quite attractive. When I came to this country in 1914, however, workers on the Pennsylvania Railroad were earning only ten cents an hour, for ten hours a day which equalled a dollar a day — but there was not much steady work.

Because there was no great prosperity when I arrived I went to New York where all the others went. There were easily 400 or 500 Sardinians in New York at the time so that I met many of my compatriots. Most lived in a small section of Mulberry Street, although a number of Sardinians lived in the Bronx.

I did not encounter much in the way of an organized *padrone* at the time. In fact there was not much organization of any kind. The Italians were more or less receptive to join unions, but not the Spanish who did not know much about this country. Thus, when the union would go on strike the employers hired the Spanish workers to break the strike, a practice which I did not see very much among the Italian workers. Once in a coal town where three or four hundred Italian workers went on strike, colored people, some Mexicans and many Spanish were shipped in from New York as strikebreakers not knowing anything more than that they had a job.

I was an only child after my brother had died as a youngster, so I came to the U.S. by myself. Friends were very helpful in those days in getting a decent job. When I lived on Mulberry Street in New York City, I lived in a rooming house in which six or seven men lived in one room paying 50 to 60 cents a week to sleep. We had to get our own meals which frequently involved going to the beer garden and getting a lunch for the price of a drink. The biggest problem I faced when I first came here was getting a job because there was a depression. I was somewhat fortunate, however, because I had saved about $150 to $200 from my work on the Canal. Eventually, I went to work in the coal mines where there were already a couple of hundred Sardinian workers, mostly from Pattada. We did not have to speak English in such a situation, nor did we have to speak Italian if we could get along with the dialects. At these coal mines there were a number of Piedmontese, and others from Tuscany and Lazio (near Rome). We all got along although there was some suspicion against southern Italians.

At the outbreak of World War I as Italy entered the war, I remember a number of Italians returned to Italy. They received free passage and were encouraged to join the Italian army, especially those who had been soldiers before. In my own case, however, I decided that I did not want to become a soldier, wanting instead to continue living by myself and not be in the service. Of course, it was also possible for me to go into the army here since I was registered but I was deferred with the help of a Sicilian on the draft board who advised me that I could avoid the army if I worked in necessary employment and paid a few dollars to the right official. Working in the coal mines was considered essential work. Of course, one had to work. I remember the coal company policemen coming around and if they saw someone not working but just lounging around the shack, they would inquire. Remember, these were company towns and almost everything belonged to the company, houses, stores, the police, the whole towns. They controlled things so rigidly that if you went out on strike you would have to get out of your house within 2 hours unless you went back to work. They did not even give you a chance to get out but they would load your belongings and dump them. In the beginning we also had to buy groceries in their stores, but this did not last as other grocery stores began to appear. We thus had an opportunity to buy Italian groceries and other items.

We read various Italian newspapers. I remember *Il Progresso Italo-Americano,* and *L'Opinione* of Philadelphia. Barsotti, who organized *Il Progresso*, was an effective writer. After Mussolini bought the papers out, and they became vehicles for his views, the papers went downhill and few Italian writers remained. There used to be many good ones, but not anymore. At least the elder Pope (Generoso Pope) was sharp, but his son Fortune does not have much ability.

At the time when I worked in the mines, there was also a lot of propaganda from the anarchists who included a number of big lawyers and educated people. One who was educated and respected among them was Carlo Tresca. He was a nice guy and he was for the working man. Even the Americans liked him because he was an honest man.

I remember the Sacco-Vanzetti case. I remember contributing for their cause ten to fifteen times. Many Italians contributed. Everybody put in because they felt these were level working men. If there had been another government in Italy at the time, Sacco and Vanzetti would not have died, but Mussolini washed his hands like Pilate.

The big man in the coal mines at the time was John L. Lewis who was so powerful that he could have been president if he wanted to. During World War I the coal mines were taken over because it was vital industry. I remember the big strike of 1922. We finally went back to work in the middle of December. To my mind Lewis made a mistake then because if he had held out for a couple of weeks, the companies would have given in, but they signed a contract which did not recognize the union although the wage settlement was what the union wanted.

It was in the mines that I contracted the black lung disease. I received compensation of $196.00 a month but many others did not. At that time mining was not as it is today. The companies then cared for no one. Precautions against the smoke and poor health conditions were minimal until the unions forced the companies to provide adequate ventilation. Newer, cleaner explosives were developed. Now the mines are much better taken care of than before. The hours are also different. We used to go in at two or three in the morning. Once, I went into the mine at one o'clock in the morning and worked until 6:00 p.m. the next evening. I was a young man and could take it, but it was hard work.

We also had religious services. There was a Catholic priest and church in town. The priest at Windber was Italian, Don Antonio, and the services were in that language. There also was an Italian priest available at Johnstown. The different nationalities had their own churches. The Poles had theirs, Italians theirs, etc. On Sundays they were all filled. At that time people went to church more regularly than today and everybody contributed a little to help support it whether five cents, ten cents, twenty-five cents, or whatever they could afford. There were many Irish priests also and there were a number of Protestant churches.

When I first came to this country I noticed there was the same separation among the Italians from different regions that there had been in Italy, with Calabrese on one side and Sicilians on another. The companies encouraged this separation because they did not want any trouble and fighting between the two. In one town I worked in, there were two streets. On Main Street all the residents were Sardinians, Tuscans or Piedmontese, and the other street was populated mostly by Calabrese from the town of Catanzaro. These people were generally quieter than those from Reggio, Calabria. At that time they got along with the Sardinians pretty well.

In politics, the company was on the lookout for those who spoke English well and generally gave them more favored positions and then encouraged them to vote. The idea was that they could count on your vote because they did you favors. Although there were no Italian political organizations in the mining town, there were other societies. One was *Figli di Italia* (Sons of Italy) with over 300 members.

When I came to Port Washington there was a Sardinian society in which I served as president for three terms. I went to Italy in 1932, stayed eight months and came back to Port Washington in 1933. In that Long Island town there were a number of my townspeople and friends including 25 families from Pattada alone in Port Washington. There were a number of Italian organizations there and we used to celebrate our big feasts like the one just before Labor Day which would last for three days. People came from all over New York and New Jersey, to eat, drink and listen to the music. We also had the cooperation of the town officials and the company which employed many of our people. This was the sand and gravel company that was later bought out by Generoso Pope and became the Colonial Sand and Gravel Company. During Generoso Pope's time, the union came and many Sardinians were involved in organizing the workers. Mr. Pope accepted us right away and said "Why didn't you come to me before. We like the union". As a result our wages improved. Of course we did have a couple of strikes later on in the 1930s, which were a bit rough as management brought in some toughs to intimidate us. A couple of guys went to the hospital but they came back after they recuperated. Now the people who work in the sand pit make big money and have easy work. I worked there until I was 74 years old, when I retired.

The Icanusa Society, our Sardinian Society, had some small benefits for members when they were sick. They also endorsed political candidates for local office and thereby had some influence. We could not get just anything we wanted but we did have some influence.

We did not have much criminal activity in Port Washington. There was no Mafia there. There wasn't much of this kind of activity in the coal mining regions I lived in either.

There was discrimination against the Italians in a number of places especially in the mines. In many companies when they found out you were Italian, they would then ask whether you were from the northern or southern part of Italy. If you were from the north, they would give you a job right away. If you were from the southern part of Italy, it was much more difficult. Many companies did not want people from the south working in their mines. Often if I would hear of a good mine to work in, I would go there and apply for a job. As soon as they heard I was from the south I would not get the job. The Sardinians were a bit better off, however, because we were neither from the north nor from the south, so we did not receive the full brunt of discrimination. Moreover the Sardinians gained a reputation as good workers. There is no question that Sardinians were good working people — like big jackasses. Today, of course, it is different and southern Italians in this country know the customs and practices well enough not to suffer such discrimination.

My best recollections of going through the immigrant experience were during World War I when I was working steadily and nobody bothered me. I had a good time among the Tuscans, Piedmontese and Lazio people who got along well with the Sardinians. On Saturdays we would have dances among the different groups or we would play *briscola, mora,* poker, or *bocci.*

The Sardinian people in Port Washington held great respect for people in authority, such as judges, senators and congressmen. If one of their own was in that position, he would get great support and respect in Port Washington. Once in awhile I go to visit in Port Washington but not so frequently anymore. I am not altogether well and need medication. Besides at one time I had many friends who drove, but now no one drives anymore and it is hard to get around.

Originally, our family (paternal name of Pieracci, maternal name Piacentini) had their roots deep in the soil of a tiny Italian village, high in the northern Apennines. Our home was in the village Frassinoro, meaning golden ash tree, in the province of Modena. The surrounding land was poor and rocky. Its people were peasants who managed to scratch only a part of their living from the unyielding soil. Each family's ancestors had cleared a few small fields where they grew a bit of wheat for their bread and some feed for a few cows, sheep and goats. From the milk they made cheese and that, along with the bread and *polenta,* was almost their whole sustenance in winter. The short summer brought a few vegetables to vary the monotony of the winter meals.

In these small villages there simply was no means of livelihood, as was the case throughout most of Italy. In winter, the men were forced to emigrate to neighboring countries to find work to support their families. The mothers cared for the babies; the young boys for the few head of livestock; and even the young girls went to the city and worked as domestics in the homes of the wealthy. The grandfathers no doubt dozed by the fireplace, while the grandmothers knitted socks and the warm woolen undergarments needed in the cold climate of that area. In spring, the men returned to help sow the small fields and help with many other chores. They stayed until the harvest when they would leave again.

My mother, Filomena (Piacentini) was a seamstress and went to neighboring villages to sew for well-to-do families. She and a friend walked from village to village with portable sewing machines strapped on their backs. It was hard work and the pay was small. My father, Orlando

Pieracci, was fourteen years of age and not yet a man when he too had to emigrate to earn money to help his family, since his father showed no inclination to leave his native village. His father, Natale Pieracci chose to make a living by plying his trade as a saddle maker but, to quote an uncle, "saddles were not in much demand, so my father made a saddle about as often as a Pope died". My father's mother Rosalia Pieracci had a small shop in the home to earn a few *centisimi*. Most every home in the village had a tiny shop or *bottega* of some sort. None really made any profit. They had to buy from each other, because each one stocked only a few items.

My father emigrated first to Scotland. He was apprenticed for five years to a man, also an Italian, who owned a chain of ice cream stores. The five years soon became fourteen and by that time he was part owner of a "fish and chips" shop.

During those years in Scotland he lived in Glasgow and Edinburgh. He worked hard and dutifully sent money home to help support his parents, several brothers and a sister. After such a long absence from his family and native village, he was persuaded to return to Italy. While in Scotland he had learned to speak English and taught himself to read and write it as well. During the years of his absence the village had not changed. It was an ancient village. The church, once an ancient monastery, was 900 years old. Since he still found no opportunity for any profitable employment, it soon became apparent that he would have to emigrate again. He did stay home for several years, however, earning a meager living by going to the city and bringing back supplies of wood and wine for the villagers. The route was over rough and treacherous mountain roads with a large wagon drawn by a pair of mules. He was not happy there and prepared to leave again, planning to return to Scotland. Fate, however, had decreed otherwise.

Since he returned, he had married and, having read and heard so much about America and of the wonderful opportunities and the freedom there, he decided to come to America instead. From the books he had read about this new land and from so far away it seemed to him that it surely must be "the land of beginning again" where he would realize his dream of a better way of life for himself and his children, for by this time there was a baby daughter.

He emigrated to America in the year 1907, which is said to have been the year of the greatest immigration influx in the history of the United States. He had only passage money for himself so he had to leave his wife and daughter behind, with the promise to send for them as soon as possible. His destination was the state of Iowa. There, near the state capital of Des

Moines, were several small coal mines. He settled in one of the camps near a mine. It was a small coal field and the coal veins were so low the men had to work on their knees or with bent backs to dig out the coal. Despite his thriftiness, and his sacrifices, it was two years before he could send for his wife and daughter.

The mining camps were quite a contrast to the mountain village in the "old country". They were all alike: clusters of small boxlike houses made of wood and painted gray, or boxcar red. These immigrants had never seen wooden houses before and they appeared flimsy indeed in comparison to the ancestral homes of stone with walls twenty inches thick. What was even more strange was the absence of trees and shrubbery for this mining camp had been built in the middle of what had been an Iowa cornfield. They were amazed at the flatness of the terrain and among themselves they called it "The Sahara". It was so far from Italy and all so strange and different. There was a great nostalgia for the "hills of home" but here they had to stay for they did not have passage money to return, and they knew they had to adjust to their new environment. In time, most of them did. The only thing that was the same as home was the bitter cold of the winters and the deep snows. They had to walk to work and although roads and paths were not cleared in winter, they rarely missed a day's work. They could not afford to. Nearly all had borrowed passage money that had to be paid back.

None of these immigrants had ever worked in the dangerous blackness of a coal mine. Consequently, every new miner was assigned to an experienced miner for several weeks. After that they were on their own, for better or worse. In the years to come many of those young immigrant miners who had come with such high hopes for a better life were crushed to death under falls of slate and stone. My father was very fortunate and he was a cautious worker who took no chances. Yet, when he left early in the morning, we were never sure he would come back alive. He spent forty years working in several Iowa coal mines — in which he saw little of either the seasons or his children.

By the year 1912 there were four children. The three youngest were born in America. The third born was a son and my father vowed that this boy would never work in a coal mine. My father had faith that this must be the land of opportunity, if not for himself, at least for his children. He made a valiant effort to better his own lot by taking a correspondence course, hoping to learn some phase of coal mining other than digging the coal. He had hoped to get a job "on top" and aspired to be at least a "check weighman", but that was not to be. Several years after the birth of the fourth child, my mother had, what is now called a tubal pregnancy and it required surgery to save her life. While the surgery was called successful, it is believed she went into shock when she learned surgery was necessary. She was the first of her family ever to be hospitalized. She had a great fear of doctors since in Italy doctors were available only in the cities. The villages had only a midwife and perhaps not even one of those. In Italy, only the strongest survived. I had heard my father say once, that Frassinoro did have a doctor. Doctors then, however, had only a little learning which was considered good enough for the peasants, who probably would not have trusted even the most learned doctor. Ignorance and superstition were prevalent then, not only in Italy, but all over the world.

After two weeks in a hospital far from the mining camp our mother came home again. If it had been a traumatic experience for us, I can only imagine what it must have been for her. We were yet babies and needed our mother very much. Her recovery, my father told us seemed good the first few months. Physically, she was soon strong again, but it was soon evident that emotionally she was troubled. Within a few years, the mind of the good wife and loving mother shut out reality until she was no longer able to function as a mother. She grieved constantly for her native land. Her nostalgia knew no reason. She had, as all immigrants, left behind beloved parents, brothers, sisters and friends. She was never to see them again, and she remained all of her life a stranger in a strange land. For many years we kept her at home, praying for a miracle that would bring our mother "back" to us. It never came. They said someday we would understand.

So it was that tragedy first came into our home in this new land. My mother was a brilliant, sensitive and devout woman and she was, until then, as our father told us, a good and loving mother. The children had not the privilege of thus remembering her. They were too young.

This all happened while living in our first mining camp — a camp which did not so much as have a grocery store or even a "company store". Most of the miners, like my parents, had come from small villages in Europe where almost every family had a small shop. Once or twice weekly mobile grocery stores would come through the camps. They were large horse-drawn wagons without ice in summer to keep the foods from spoiling. In winter things froze but we were still able to buy many of the foods native to this land. I especially remember the whole salted cod fish because it never spoiled winter or summer. The Italians call it *baccala*. My father would chop off a piece with a hatchet. It was soaked to remove salt, boiled until tender and tomatoes were added and simmered for a time. Meanwhile he would make a big golden yellow *polenta*. When done it was turned out on a board, cut into steaming slices with a heavy string and served with the *baccala*. We were fortunate to have crusty delicious Italian bread brought in from a wagon from another mining camp that had an Italian bakery. It was a bit of Italy in America for them. Some of the miners made their own wine with grapes shipped in from California and, as the years went on, while they accepted other American ways and things their food preferences always remained Italian.

In winter, the wells froze and water had to be drawn and stored in pails for the next day. If there were snow or icicles, these were melted and heated to pour on the frozen pumps. Not only was the water situation bad in winter, but in the summer the wells would almost dry up. Sometimes there was only enough for cooking and drinking. For washing, the coal company brought "steam water" from the mine. It came in large horse-drawn tanks. I still remember the women and children going out to the tanks with all sorts of containers to get this wash water. From the road it had to be carried to the house then heated on a coal burning stove called a "range". For the menfolk, sometimes the "beer man" came with beer, that could be cooled only with well water, when there was enough of that. My father, strangely enough, for an Italian, would not drink anything alcoholic, not even wine at meals. I am sure life would have been even harder for us had my father spent his hard earned money for beer and wine which was expensive even then.

Most families, except ours, managed to take in at least two male boarders. These were mostly single men who came to America to "seek their fortune" but, like my father, got only as far as these small Iowa coal fields. In most of those little four room houses, three of the four small rooms were bedrooms. The kitchen served also as a dining room and the boarders ate with the family. There were, naturally, no restaurants. Most camps did have one large home, called a boarding house, but they were always filled to capacity. As the families began to increase they were crowded and miserable. The houses, had no porches, and no closets or basements. They were cheaply constructed wooden shells which became bitterly cold in winter and stifling hot in summer. The heating stove heated poorly, the one room it was in, since bituminous coal does not throw much heat. Also, this coal contains much sulphur, so our air was heavily polluted. With the coal dust the miners breathed in while at work and the sulphur fumes at home it is no wonder many suffered from black lung disease. Even now I cannot forget the cold of those years during the severe Iowa winters. There never seemed to be quite enough warm bedding or clothing. Had our mother been able to sew and knit for us it might have been different, for she had been a seamstress and had even been able to tailor men's clothing, when a young woman, before the "sickness" came. So my father had to go to the city of Des Moines, by train on Saturday afternoons to buy our clothing ready made and our shoes without knowing our foot size. The children could not go. Our shoes seldom fit and my father's choice of our dresses and coats left much to be desired. Actually, we did not really suffer by comparison because the other fathers did no better.

In those years my father also learned how to repair our shoes. As soon as he had finished one, we would put it on right away while the inside was still warm from the pounding of the hammer on the shoe soles. One of our few happy memories is that feeling of warmth inside our shoes after father finished soling them. They may have pinched our feet and crowded our toes, but at least we did not go barefooted unless we wanted to. Because of my father's many years in Scotland he spoke beautiful English with a heavy Scottish "burr" and was often called upon to act as interpreter. Usually it was when the doctor was needed. Nearly always it was when a new baby was born. The nearest and only telephone was at the mine which was quite a distance from our home. It was my father who had to go to call the doctor, because the other immigrants had not yet learned to speak any English. It was not until their children were old enough to go to school that the parents learned even a bit of English, which they still found difficult. As time went on, the children forgot the native tongue and the parents did not or could not learn English, resulting in a communication gap between these immigrant parents and their American born children. The parents desired an education for their children, and they knew that with an education their children would not have to labor in the dark tunnels of a coal mine. A better way of life had been their dream in the old country and they knew it would be realized here in America. The immigrant parents would be more or less a "lost generation", but they seemed not to regret it or feel bitter for they had gained much in the migration process. Now their children and their children's children would probably never know as the parents had, hunger and oppression and, best of all, they would have the opportunity to learn.

Now, we hear songs in December about "Christmas in the City" and sleigh bells ringing and children so happy. Only the child of an immigrant, however, can know or remember Christmas in a mining camp. My father had told us about the Italian Santa Claus who was a woman called *La Befana.* My two little sisters and brother were too young to understand, or to remember this now. My father would go to the city for Christmas shopping, but his pay did not allow him to buy very much. The night before Christmas, he would hang up for us, brightly colored knitted stockings, made by our grandmother and brought to America by another villager. On Christmas morning — the American Christmas morning — the *Befana* had left each of us a ten cent toy, an orange, a Hershey almond bar, and a pair of stockings or some much needed garment. Sometimes there would be chestnuts to roast or boil. The bread man usually brought every family a coffee bread called *panettone.* This was a great treat because it was sweet and had raisins in it. We had no Christmas tree. No one made us Christmas cookies. No one brought Christmas baskets full of good things to these immigrant families. There was no turkey and "all the trimmin's". In the first years there was not even chicken. For Christmas dinner we would have a big pot of soup with *ditalini,* sprinkled with Parmesan cheese. This was prepared by our father.

At school, after the usual Christmas program, the mine owner usually furnished an orange or an apple for each child. Candy at Christmas was unknown to us until many years later, and we did not learn until our early teens that Christmas day was the birthday of the Christ child. This mining camp had no church of any kind. Most of the immigrants had been Catholic in Italy, and still considered themselves good Catholics even if they could not worship or participate in the rituals of their religion. Many years later in different locations and with the advent of the automobile these people and most of the children returned to the religion of their forefathers.

During the years we lived in our first mining camp, six or seven young miners of different nationalities were killed by falls of slate. One can only imagine the sorrow of their families across the sea, when they received the sad news often months after the tragedy. While there was no dangerous gas in these small Iowa mines, the ceiling was extremely treacherous and, if not propped up correctly, the slate would often crush the unfortunate miner to death. A mine fatality was announced by the shriek of a siren, heard all over the camp. The women would grab up the babies and run to the mine, each praying it was not her husband who had been killed. Shortly afterwards the miners would come up and it was soon learned who had lost his life. It was a sad unforgettable sight and sound. The young family was so bereft and now so alone in this new land. In time, a miner's widow might remarry, but until that time she had to be the breadwinner. In the mining camp all she could do was take in boarders. There was no insurance money and no financial help from the coal company. She would not even have the funds to enable her to return to Italy where her family would help out.

In 1916 we moved to another small mining camp several miles away, my father prompted by the thought that perhaps this might benefit our mother. The move was also necessitated by the slackening in this vein of coal. This next mining camp was almost a replica of the first, and how happy we were to learn that here at least there were two stores nearby. One store carried the imported food staples appreciated by the immigrant miners and the other was a company store with American foods. There was even a farm close by where we could get fresh milk and eggs. In many ways it was easier living here, but my mother's condition did not improve. As a result, we children learned early to do for ourselves.

At ten years of age, I was still too young to help a great deal. My father prepared his own breakfast and packed a lunch which he ate in the mine by the light of his carbide lamp. The lunch was almost always two sandwiches, one of which was salami and the other brick cheese. No doubt by noon they were both dry and musky. The top tray of the miner's pail held these sandwiches while the bottom half held about one gallon of water which often had to be taken from home. Sometimes in summer there might also be an apple from a nearby farm. In this town we could get store cookies so that was the dessert. The children were close enough to school to be able to come home for lunch. My father had to get up earlier than most of the miners, so he could make a pot of porridge or cream of wheat for our breakfast. He poured it into four bowls and when we arose, if there was milk in the house, we poured a bit over the now cold breakfast. In summer, if we forgot to boil the milk the night before, by morning it was spoiled. That was before my father learned about canned milk. This was good for our coffee and kept longer. These were desperate years for us and like Topsy "we jes grew"; nevertheless, we had no serious illnesses or accidents. The life of most of these immigrants was, up to now, not much easier than in Europe. Since they knew life here would be better for their children, no sacrifice was too great an effort to see the fulfillment of their dream of that better way of life.

Education to my father was almost an obsession. Like the father of Fannie Hurst, the famous Jewish novelist, "education was all". To be late or absent from school was, at our house, considered almost a sin. My father having schooled himself to some extent while living in Scotland was, in many ways, more progressive than some of the other miners. We had the first oilstove and the first linoleum in that mining camp. We had to learn to cook as soon as possible and we found the oilstove more convenient, even if we had to walk to the company store every day for a gallon of kerosene. We were constantly admonished to be very careful when using it. While clean and convenient it could also have been dangerous. Fortunately we heeded the warnings and had no accidents. Our mother was still able, to some extent, to assume some responsibility for us and was able to cook for herself, even though she had escaped from the world of reality. Medical science did not have the knowledge then to help and this "sickness" brought us heartaches that no others can ever know who have not had it in their home.

It was here in our second mining camp that we saw Negroes for the first time. A few Negro families lived here in this camp and were coal miners too, but I do not remember any prejudice shown them by the immigrants or their children. We were both members of minority groups against whom there was prejudice. We learned no prejudice in our home and we did not hear the names "Nigger", "Wop", "Dago" or "Polack" until we moved again to yet another mining camp, several years later.

In the second mining camp came my first encounter with what I learned later was called religion. I did not know before this why babies were taken to the city to be baptized. I was born in Italy and baptized there but did not know it in those young years. I always accompanied my parents each time one of the younger children was baptized, but I did not know what it meant. I remember the dark interiors of what I learned later were Catholic Churches, the lighted candles, the baptismal font, and seeing the ceremony performed by a man in a lace robe. Afterward we all walked to a photographer to have group pictures taken. Also present were the godfather and godmother. Our mode of transportation was still the train. This ride was another of the few good memorable experiences for me. Our mother was still well until after the birth of the fourth and last child. In one of the group baptismal pictures she proudly holds her baby son baptized that day so long ago. She was happy then. Several years later, however, happiness left our home when it became necessary to hospitalize her for long periods of time. It was difficult for us to understand, but my father knew he must gather courage anew and go on for the sake of his children.

When I was about eleven years old, two ladies came from the city and gathered up the children of Catholic families and conducted Sunday

School in the schoolhouse. This, I learned, was called "catechism". We attended every Sunday. I remember learning my lessons well and being rewarded with a beautiful rosary. Still I did not know what it all meant. In a few months several older members of the class were told we were ready for our First Communion. The teachers were to bring me a white dress for the occasion. We were to be taken to the city church for the ceremony. On a warm and beautiful Sunday morning, we assembled at the schoolhouse to await the teachers and I was anxious to see the white dress they were bringing for me. I had never had a white dress, since a coal miner's wage could not be stretched or spent for such luxuries. Also, there had never really been an occasion to wear one. The children waited several hours, but the teachers never came. I remember that morning as one of my first disappointments. Sadly we returned home and because there were no phones and no American newspapers came to the camp until much later, we did not know what had happened. They did not come the next Sunday, nor the next. Then came the tragic news that our good catechism teachers had been killed in some sort of accident a few days before the Sunday that was to have been our First Communion. This sadly ended our religious instructions, so it was not until we were adults that we learned what religion was. One of my sisters called that period, "the great void in our life" and indeed it was, but the same could be said about all who lived in those places and who had come here as immigrants. Those who settled in the large cities have a different story to tell about every aspect of their life in America, I am sure. How often I have wished that our father could have escaped the bitter cold of the winters in Iowa. Again, however, fate decreed otherwise and here we have remained, except for one sister who moved some years ago.

When I was about twelve years of age my father decided to take us away from the environment of the mining camps. Because he had no other skills, however, it could not be too far from one. He finally found a small acreage on the edge of another mining camp. It was about seven acres of rich Iowa farm land. The few acres were worked by a farmer on shares. My father was also able to have a big garden and have the fruit trees and the rose arbor that had been part of his dream of a better way of life. Here we had a nicer home, with an upstairs. Our new home was painted white. Mining camp homes were never painted white. My father fenced in the small piece of land. Soon we had a lawn and a cement sidewalk and a white gate with purple lilac bushes on each side. There were no shade trees, but we children went on flower picking expeditions along the railroad tracks. Here we found young poplar trees, pulled them up and planted them beside the house. In a few years we had shade. We were enchanted in summer to hear the rustle of the leaves of trees. This was not rented property. This was all our own. My father worked hard to pay for that land and here, in America, it was possible to buy a piece of land. Despite the hardships, my father loved not only the land, but he loved the country. It was now his adopted country and the proudest day of his life was, I believe, the day he received his American citizenship papers. Two Jewish merchants from the city of Des Moines, from whom my father purchased much of our furniture and clothing, were his witnesses at the ceremony.

Now, as the oldest child I was finally old enough to assume many of the household chores that had been performed for us by my father. I learned how to cook and wash. I now got up early in the morning to prepare my father's breakfast and pack his lunch pail. Later my two younger sisters shared in these household duties, so it was a bit easier for my father. During the school year and the winter, however, it was still very difficult, and it was not the carefree time of life it should have been. Although we were only entering our teens, we carried the burdens of adults.

The third mining camp was near our new home. In appearance it was exactly like the others consisting of small gray miners' shacks set near a farming community. Iowa was and still is predominately agricultural although it has become quite industrialized since World War II. The small coal fields in the Des Moines area were of little consequence and in a few years they played out one by one. The former site of the mining camp is now an industrial park. Now, as I pass by the site on a modern paved road in a modern motor car, I see again the camp I knew as a child, with the little Italian store and the company store where the miners could charge their groceries and payment was deducted from their wages at the mine. I see again the little gray schoolhouse so crowded with children and so poorly equipped. Here, one teacher taught all subjects to eight grades. It was amazing how much the children learned even under such circumstances. No doubt the same could be said about all of the "little red schoolhouses". We were eager students and books were precious. We had little to read except textbooks and the *Miners Journal* and since my father read English, we did take an English newspaper which we literally devoured. We all finished grade school here which was quite an accomplishment considering the turmoil of our family and the dim lighting of the kerosene lamp. I often wonder now, how one of us became the school's spelling champion. It was with great pride my father accompanied that child, his only son, to the county spelling match. Even though he did not win first prize it was honor enough for us.

We thoroughly enjoyed the acreage home. There was a lot of room to play in, but we had only a few playmates from a neighboring farm. The children from the mining camp did not come down and we were not allowed to go there, except to school and to the store. Because of my mother's illness it was best that there not be noisy children around the house. Nor could we have neighborly visitors. Consequently, we were shy and withdrawn when we found ourselves among people.

It was here that we were, for the first time, called "Wop", "Dago" and "white trash", by the Negroes living in and around the mining camp. At school they threatened us and often threw rocks at us. We were frightened of them, but we soon learned that those children were in the minority and most of the families did not allow their children to abuse the white children or call them names. Many became our friends, and those still living have remained faithful friends through the years. They shared the hardships and the poverty with the immigrant whites. These families were only a few generations removed from slavery.

As we graduated one by one, from the small mining camp school, we attended high school in a small town several miles away. We reached it by going on an interurban train, that passed only a few blocks from our home. When my father had three children in high school at once, often there was not enough car fare for all so they walked the distance of two miles to high school. The children from the farm homes had their own school several miles from the mining camp, and the parents took them there by horse and buggy. They were prejudiced against the recent immigrants of a different ethnic group. Although they were "Americans" they too were only a generation or two removed from foreign soil. Their ancestors had come to these shores for the same reason as ours, but they chose not to remember.

We were still on the acreage when we all graduated from high school. The high school years were extremely difficult for all of us. Financially it was hard on my father. He had to try to dig out and load more coal to enable him to keep four children in school. His years in Scotland had no doubt taught him to admire the thriftiness of the Scottish and already having a goodly measure of his own, he was never without a few dollars tucked away in the bank. He prized his credit and never purchased anything, except groceries, unless he could pay cash.

As each child graduated from high school my father was extremely proud. It was a great achievement for all. No doubt he was a little extra proud when his son graduated at the head of his class and was presented with a silver loving cup and a small scholarship by the local American Legion Post. Immigrant parents whose children had graduated from high school found it difficult to believe that with so much education the graduate could not find gainful employment. Consequently some of the sons went into the coal mines with their fathers. Many of the daughters married early or had, as their ancestors, gone to the city to work as domestics or in the small factories in the area. While I chose to stay home and care for my mother whom we had returned to the home, the other children chose to go on to college. They knew they would have to work their way through. Except for an occasional five or ten dollars, my father could not help. The other children went on to college under the most adverse conditions. Hard times had indeed come upon this new land of opportunity. The depression of the thirties was a shattering blow to the hopes and dreams of these people but they were not strangers to poverty, so they made the best of it and rode it out in stride. The children who went to college did not drop out. To their everlasting credit they remained and in due time they graduated. Each graduation was another proud day in my father's life. When the immigrant parents saw that their own children could go to college, they knew that the better way of life had finally been realized. As each one went out into the world and achieved various degrees of success, they basked in reflected glory.

My father saw his son become an electrical engineer and later acquire more college credit and degrees. Two daughters became school teachers. All married and established homes and families of their own, but he was granted only brief glimpses of two of his grandchildren.

In the late thirties my father was still working in the mines. One day the small mine became flooded and had to be abandoned. Since there were no other mines within walking distance, it became necessary for him to commute to a mine about thirty miles away. Commuting was almost an unheard of thing in those days since most of the mining camps were in the shadow of the mine.

We continued to live on the acreage for quite a few years longer. Eventually, however, the other children who had left the paternal home to pursue a life of their own, persuaded my father to sell the acreage and move to the small town where we had gone to high school. Here, the homes were modern and we would have electric lights, central heating and, best of all, an inside bathroom. My father was reluctant to move, but finally we did move into town where we were fortunate to find a nice little five room bungalow, in a desirable location. This was indeed a better way of living. Our ancestors would never have even dreamed of such convenience and luxury. While it was not really luxurious it seemed most wonderful to us, mostly because of the modern convenience. My father and I were both avid readers and now the electric light would make reading much more pleasurable. In this home we also had a furnace that kept all the rooms warm day and night, and the house had storm windows of glass, instead of the black tar paper that was used in the mining camp to keep out the bitter cold winds of Iowa winters.

At this time my father was still working at a mine about thirty miles away, so he decided to purchase and learn to drive a car. With the financial help of a brother, he bought a Model T Ford, and courageously set about learning to drive. The pick and shovel, however, were more familiar to his hands than the steering wheel, and he had a few minor accidents before turning the driving chore over to his brother. Several other miners rode with them to the new mine. It was to be the last mine my father ever worked in. Several years later, my father came home at noon, I was frightened even though I saw he was not injured, I thought he had become ill in the mine, but that also was not the case. While I was exceedingly thankful, I knew then it was because a man had been killed. My father dropped his lunch pail to the floor and with tears in his eyes he told me it was one of the men who rode in his car. A boy of only eighteen years, he had been crushed to death by a fall of slate. My father was griefstricken. The boy's parents were also Italian immigrants and friends of ours. My father's thoughts perhaps were that but for the grace of God, that could have been his own son.

That day my father quit working in the mine. He said he could not go back. After almost forty years of back breaking work in the coal mines, where no sunlight ever penetrated, he was tired. He had shovelled many tons of coal. He had endured great hardships and made many sacrifices to achieve his dream. Yet, he was not given many more years to bask in that reflected glory of his children's success. From the beginning of his new way of life in this promised land there had been anxieties and heartaches that added to the burden he carried. All of this had taken its toll on his health, and it was with great sadness that we watched him fail and languish, often in pain which he tried to hide from us. He had been strong and was a handsome man with Lincolnesque features, and a dry sense of humor.

On March 14, 1947, our father, Orlando Pieracci was gone. Our sorrow knew no bounds. He was 69 years old.

Our mother, Filomena Pieracci lived for fifteen more years. She was then 84 years of age. Our mother never gave up hope that someday she would again see her native village and all of those familiar faces. The letters from the old country always told her how they longed to see her again.

One March day in 1964, she went away, "gently, in her sleep" they said. She was laid to rest beside her husband and in her hand we placed a packet of soil from her native village.

Going through some old letters I came across the following poem. It is not from the *Miners Journal,* but perhaps, at some time or other, it has appeared there. Regretfully, I do not know the author.

The Miners' Prayer

Oh, God of hosts, our shield and tower,
Display Thy mercy and Thy power,
Protect all workers underground
And spread Thy shelt'ring wings around.
And hear us in Thy love divine
For those in peril in the mine.

When to the darkness depths below
For daily bread to toil they go,
Where feeble lights are dimly thrown,
And dangers lurk unseen, unknown,
Lord hear us in Thy power divine
For those in peril in the mine.

From falling roof or stone or beam,
Explosive gas or scalding steam,
From fire and water, dust and damp,
Oh! God be Thou their safety lamp.
And hear us in Thy power divine
For those in peril in the mine.

Oh those whom death called from their task,
Their blessing, gracious God, we ask;
That each may see his Savior's face,
May know His sovereign, saving grace.
Tendrils of love our hearts entwine,
For those who perish in the mine.

~TWO ~
The Shoemakers

Introduction

Few economic activities demonstrated the disparity of public esteem between Italy and the United States as that accorded to the craft of shoemaking. While the craft may have merited some degree of favorable acknowledgement in an earlier America, its luster lessened in the heyday of mass industrialization prevalent in the early twentieth century. Increasingly, shoemaking came to be regarded as a field entered by those of little ambition who, having become inured to the simple and the familiar avoided the challenges of more progressive pursuits.

In Italy, by contrast, the shoemaker had always enjoyed a position as an indispensable factor in the life of the community. It was one of the crafts one could learn only through long apprenticeship and, when mastered, guaranteed the master a fairly secure economic existence. Furthermore, in the absence of real opportunity for higher education, the craft was cherished as a sought-after occupation worthy of both the practitioner and his family.

For the classical shoemaker, the making of the entire shoe, from the selection of leather to the insertion of shoelaces was his undertaking. It was necessary for him to know the characteristics of various leathers and be familiar enough with the human anatomy to make appropriate allowances for individual physical features. The Italian shoemaker came by his skills after serving a customary apprenticeship which might last several years. In a word the Italian shoemakers were Old World craftsmen, participating in a tradition that extended back hundreds of years.

From the beginning of the extensive Italian immigration to the United States, shoemakers constituted a substantial portion of the skilled labor as thousands of Italian men attempted to transplant their craft to the new country believing that it afforded a favorable means of earning a living, especially when compared to the unskilled positions given their fellow countrymen. Once settled in the United States they plied their trade either as individual proprietors of small shops, or as workers in large manufacturing companies. The small Italian owned shoemaker shop was a common feature in every Italian neighborhood with some shoemakers passing their trade from father to son to grandson.

This was the background of two of the individuals whose careers as shoemakers marked their entry into American life. Alert, knowledgeable and intelligent, these men provide a formidable argument against the stereotype of the "ignorant" shoemakers. The first, Henry Tolino of Brooklyn, worked his craft in some of the large American shoe manufacturing plants while the second, Remigio Pane, worked in the smaller shops in New Jersey. Both were interested in organizing their fellow shoemakers and both went on to other careers following their years in the shoemaking industry.

Henry Tolino, now in his seventies was voluble and exuberant as he discussed his life, first as a shoemaker's apprentice and then as a first-class craftsman. Providing fascinating insight into the place and the role of shoemakers in his native land, he described a trade that was highly regarded among his countrymen.

Remigio Pane has had a truly remarkable career. Entering the United States as an immigrant, he worked for a number of years in the shoemaking trade in which he achieved a measure of success. Pane's interests, however, went beyond shoe craft and he finally completed an extensive college education which had been begun in night school. Later, he proceeded to become a professor of Italian at Rutger's University where he has remained for the last thirty-nine years. In the course of that tenure he introduced the study of Italian and developed it into one of the nation's leading college language programs. As chairman of the department he guided its growth until now at which time the department carries over one hundred graduate students and is one of the largest language departments in the nation. Pane remains active and interested in the developments in his field and continues to provide for his students a generous expertise as they explore the Italian language and culture.

Henry Tolino

My father's was a prominent family who owned property on the Flume di Calore (Warm River) located in the province of Avellino in the state of Naples. In spite of the wealth and prestige attached to his family in Italy, my father decided to emigrate to the United States. As a republican, he felt he could not endure living under the Italian monarchy and he was determined to leave Italy for America where his children would be allowed to choose their own way of life.

My mother's home town was different from my father's home town and, although only a few miles apart, they had two different cultures. Also, my father's family were agriculturists, while my mother's tended to be professionals, especially oriented towards theology. The monsignor by whom I was baptized was a member of my mother's family. There were also a number of priests in my father's family.

My father came to the United States in 1910 while my mother, brother and two sisters remained in Italy. A year after his arrival in 1911, Italy began drafting young men into the army. There were six sons in my father's family who did not look forward to spending so many years in the Italian army without learning a trade and this discouraged him from returning to Italy.

In Italy each student was also expected to learn a trade, regardless of his professional plans, so he would always have employment to fall back on. Thus, the first four years of elementary school were devoted to general education. Beginning with the fifth grade each would study a skilled trade for a few years. Then, if you wished to enter a profession you would undertake your studies.

I began to learn the shoemaking trade in Italy when I was six years old. The craft of shoemaking was learned from the bottom up. As an apprentice, we would take shoes apart to learn how to make the shoe patterns for women, children, and men. Each aspect of shoemaking was a specialty in itself, and bootmaking required still different techniques.

When my family first arrived in the United States we settled on Union Street in Brooklyn since it was here that our uncles, aunts, relatives and friends who had preceeded us to America lived. Since it was not a question of money which prompted my family to emigrate we would never have come as pioneers. We knew what we were coming for and if we did not like the life here we were prepared to return to Italy. Before leaving Italy I was able to study a little English. I had a cousin in our home town who had been to America and who described America to us. "In America", he would say, "you are considered equal to anybody else and need not let anybody bulldoze you. In America you are equal and there is nobody better than you. You are a man as you are and you are to be respected and you respect others." A number of townspeople had come to America but some of them returned to Italy for one reason or another. My cousin had the misfortune of not having anyone to pave the way for him. Consequently, he went to Mulberry Street which proved too confining for him. He never saw much of America beyond the city ghetto and felt it was too much of a trap.

I was about twelve or thirteen when we came to this country and I had seven or eight years apprenticeship in shoemaking. Thus, after school hours I would bicycle to a store at 1365 Flatbush Avenue which repaired women's fine shoes. There, the owner would set apart two or three pairs of shoes for me to mend. I would make the repairs by hand, sewing for the most part, and return home at about 7:00 p.m. or even 9:00 p.m.

When I came from Italy I had already gone to grade four in school. So, in America, they had a difficult time deciding in what grade I belonged, since I knew my lessons in Italian.

We were twelve in my family. My mother had had three sets of twins, a pair of which had come to live in this country. My brothers and sisters came here first with my father; then after a couple of years, we came. My father saw the approach of World War I and decided to send for the family. Through my father we were already citizens. I came in 1915, and attended P.S. 4, one of the oldest schools in Brooklyn. At the age of fifteen I joined the Navy and spent three and a half years in the service.

When I joined the Navy, my father reminded me that although I may have joined because I wanted to be with my friends, I must remember my family. He cautioned me that there had never been dishonor in the family and that I should return home only after I had earned an honorable discharge.

When I entered the Navy I was first sent to Hampton Roads, Virginia. After boot camp and a qualifying exam, I was admitted to Signal School, which lasted six months without furlough. At the school there was an American of Italian descent from Louisana who befriended me and with whom I became close friends. I used to go to the beach with him on Sundays and we would practice our signals, especially emergency signals. I did very well in Signal School considering the exam was in Latin.

Since the Signal School examination was a written one, I simply translated the words the way I read them. Later the supervisor was so surprised at how well I did, he said to me, "Why did you copy this examination?" I said "What do you mean? I put it down the way you told it to me." He had me do the test over again and again but I had it perfect because I knew Latin from my education in Italy.

Although the work in the Navy was serious there were some light moments. In Gibraltar, during a goodwill tour, I was given permission to signal an Italian warship standing by in the harbor. I asked for permission to visit the ship together with another Italian American sailor friend and we were graciously and happily welcomed. It was a source of pride to see this impressive Italian vessel, because it was a part of me and my heritage *(Questa e una cose di me).*

I stayed in the Navy Signal Corps over two years and was contemplating a longer hitch, but my mother was opposed so I left the Navy in November, 1923, and went back to the shoe line.

When I returned home I went to work first for one firm for a short period and then transferred to work for the Bernstein Brothers Shoe Company. I had previously worked for other shoe shops so I had varied experience in a number of different shoe factories. Consequently, I also served as a translator in these shops. The Jewish fellows and the Italians had difficulty reading the sizes of the shoes on the orders, so I would explain what sizes they should make for heels, soles, etc. Since the foreman only spoke English, I became very useful. Gradually, the boss became dependent upon me and used me whenever problems or complaints arose. Generally, I would defend the workers against unjust complaints and thereby began to be called "maestro" or "pop" by the employees. From settling problems within the shop in which I worked I was soon called upon to help settle disputes in other shoe shops. When workers would complain that the boss would not give additional money for making wing-tips, I had to explain to the employers that wing-tips were a long and laborious process and that they should pay for it. There were different prices for different categories of work. If you had to make a pair of plain shoes it would be worth a dollar and a half, a wing-tip would be worth a dollar and seventy five cents, an opera pump, with an open part would be two and a half dollars, etc. This difference was due to a recognition that each shoe required a different type of work. An eyelet requires one activity, while a plain shoe another; and the shoe last has to be made according to still another design. There used to be a price list for the various items but sometimes the foreman would contend that he could not meet the listing, in which case I would set him straight. Consequently, I became the head of the coordinating committee to establish an accepted price between employers and employees.

As soon as I was old enough I joined and became active in the Boot and Shoeworkers of America of the American Federation of Labor. To join this craft organization you had to pass an examination which I had passed when I was fifteen years old. Of course I was still too young then to get employment as a craftsman since you had to be 18 years old before you could get the union book enabling one to work as a craft shoemaker. After my tour in the Navy I was old enough and obtained my book right away from the American Federation of Labor. I was usually the youngest craft worker in the shop. Eventually, I was elected chairman of the overall production of the shoes since I knew the various aspects of shoemaking thoroughly.

As coordinating chairman I had an unusual role to play. I gained the confidence and goodwill of the workers who elected me and I had a special relationship with the employers who accepted me as an impartial chairman to help settle disputes which arose between the workers and the employers. In this role I had to be objective. If the management called me regarding the quality of some shoes which were produced but which were substandard, I had to be honest and say that they did not meet the standards and the workers would have to do them over again. Moreover, I would tell the worker involved that his work was below standard. Conversely, when the employers were in the wrong I did not hesitate to tell them! It was a responsible position which could get me sued if not handled properly. In fact, I was sued on one occasion but was exonerated because my role in the particular matter was very limited.

The ethnic composition of the shoeworkers in Brooklyn was largely Italian and Jewish, but the militant were usually Jewish. Some Italians followed these men whether they were right or wrong, not really knowing what they were doing. When a left-winger attempted to organize the men he usually did not succeed because he was doing it wrong. You cannot organize a group along the lines of the Socialist Party or the Communist Party if these people are skilled labor. Actually, these organizers were simply trying to use for their own purposes, the dues of the well-paid skilled workers in the shoe industry, which was among the highest paying industries at the time. This was the case with left wing leaders like Ben Gold of the Furriers Union who tried to organize skilled workers in New York. Most of these organizers were influenced by politically minded professors of the left who were not really helping the workers. They were skunks, interested only in political power and not in uplifting the workers. They wanted your gold and your life, but were prepared to put very little food on your table. They were using the workers for their own political objectives. I know about this because I was affiliated with these people in the industrial unions. At one point these independent unions called me and said "Henry, you don't belong to the American Federation of Labor; they are a bunch of thieves. You belong with us, the working class." I said, "Wait a minute. I am a worker. I believe in the working class, but not your party which is espousing a foreign, un-American ideology. I don't believe in joining such a party. I don't belong to the Sons of Italy. If I did not earn my citizenship up to now, I would not earn it by joining your party." I rejected them outright, but many less-knowledgeable in the trade followed them. The Italians were innocent, ignorant of political situations and easily influenced by propaganda. They would go on strike without any reason.

I remember one time while I was working at Bernstein Brothers shoe factory, these Communist workers struck the Martin Weinstein shop and Martin Weinstein called me in. I was excused by my employer to see what I could do about the competing labor factions, although I would not get paid for the time I was gone. Fortunately my co-workers, who were really union men, helped me out and finished my shoes so that I would not lose pay by going to help settle the dispute. We union men were considerate of each other and willing to help each other. We were working people who cared for each other. We also were proud of our workmanship and determined to give our employer the best we could.

When I went over to study the labor problems at Martin Weinstein, I spoke to the workers and they listened to me because they knew that I was not a political man. I told them to think twice before they took a serious step like a strike. "Nobody puts the bread on the table but you. But don't listen to me or to anybody but yourselves. These are the conditions and these are possible steps you can take. Which shall it be?" I also told them not to fall for political propaganda neither from the right (Mussolini) nor the left (Lenin). "We are in this country. We are stuck together. This is the way we get our bread and butter. This is the way we have bought our houses. This is the way we live. If you want to go to Mussolini, go back to Italy. If these guys like Russia so much, let them stay there!" At the same time I told them that I was not a capitalist, that I took home the same pay they did, and that I was one of them. I told them I was only speaking for myself, but I was speaking their language. They knew what I was talking about. I did not want them to take a wrong road because it would affect me also. I was in the same boat as they were. I told them about the history of the American Federation of Labor, that it had a long history and had been successfully leading the labor movement for many years and that they should listen to it. There was no need to change to a left-wing union. They had nothing to offer, I told them, "You people would change your church, what's the matter with you?"

The Communists wanted me to join them because I knew how to talk to the masses, but I could not go along with the Communists. The American Federation of Labor knew that I could settle the contract with these workers and that if I explained the kind of good contract we had at Bernstein Brothers, the workers at Martin Weinstein would understand. I told them about the advantages of our contract including a bond we put up as part of a binding agreement. In return, the management could not lock us out. We had one of the best contracts in the industry. On Jewish holidays and on Columbus Day we had off from work with pay. I was on the coordinating committee which helped to bring this about. This was before the inauguration of the National Recovery Act of Franklin D. Roosevelt. After the establishment of the NRA we had to dissolve.

The following morning I received a call from the president of my union to help settle the strike at Martin Weinstein. Filene DeNovellis was the business agent at the time. Now he is the president of the Shoeworkers Union. Girolomo Valente was the official organizer for the entire shoe industry for a number of states. Valente had come from Pennsylvania where he had been a mine worker and had then gone to Brooklyn where he became a union organizer. He was the official spokesman for the labor organization, while I was the spokesman for the workers in the trade. Finally, the workers went off the job for no reason at all. My task was to talk to the shoe manufacturers group called the Board of Trade, through their spokesman who represented 20 or 30 manufacturers. The union gave me the authority to review the situation and use my own judgment settling it. Before I went to the factory I registered with the police department because it might have been necessary to pull a strike and everything had to be cleared with the authorities. When I went to speak to the workers they told me they no longer wanted to be affiliated with the Amalgamated Manufacturers group, but wanted to join an independent union like the American Federation of Labor. I told them they could become part of the AFL but that they would have to form a local.

While these deliberations were going on, I was approached by a police captain who told me that I was wanted at the station house. I did not resist but asked what was wrong. He told me I would find out at the station house, but he also told me that I was an agitator and that they had a complaint against me! While I did not resist I told the captain that I had not just stepped off the boat and that they probably had the wrong man. Before going I recorded his number and reminded him that I knew the officer at the station house better than he did. I told him I was not a hoodlum as he suspected me of being and suggested that he was a public servant and that while he had his job to perform he had no right to insult me. Furthermore, I told him that just because he saw I was Italian, he could not just push me around because he was an Irish cop. I said that my background was just as good as his. He responded by saying that for a rebel I astonished him. I said "good", although I did not know what kind of rebel he took me for. Meanwhile, I went to the station house and they were about to book me when I warned them that they had better make sure what they were doing because they could have a million dollar law suit on their hands for the City of New York. At that point, the station lieutenant came up and said "We may have the wrong guy here." The lieutenant in fact was an old acquaintance of mine with whom I had a number of dealings over the years. Whenever he used to come over to the shop to sell tickets to the policemen's benefit, he used to see me and I would help him sell many tickets. He told the captain that he knew me and that we came from the same neighborhood and that he could vouch for me. The captain said he had picked me up on the accusation that I was a Communist agitator and troublemaker. "What? — are you crazy?" the lieutenant told the captain "This guy is a Catholic and one of the leading Catholics at St. Francis

Church. He is an usher there." He told the captain that he had the wrong guy. Actually the police had been tipped off about Rocco Franchesini who was a Communist and an agitator, but they had confused me with him. In the end, Martin Weinstein himself came down to the station house to help clear up the matter because he knew I had been sent to his shop to settle the labor dispute. If even more proof were needed, Martin Weinstein called up my boss who advised him to get me out of the station house and allow me to settle the strike. In addition he wanted it to be done right away so I could continue my work at my own shop.

Before I left I reminded that captain of his mood when he arrested me, a mood which had him about to crack me over the skull with his night stick. "Suppose you had cracked my head open and ruined me and my family. I am married and have kids. Would you have felt sorry for that? You would have destroyed me, an innocent man, because you had the power that went with being a police captain, without knowing what-the-hell you were doing. If somebody told you I had killed somebody would you shoot me? Is this what they taught you?" I told him that when I was in the Navy I was taught to obey the last order first but they had to be certain as to what that order was. I then turned to Mr. Weinstein and told him I was willing to forget the incident on the condition that the strike be settled that afternoon. Either the workers would agree to stay with the employers' Board of Trade group or they would come into the AFL. Weinstein agreed and the arrest incident was forgotten while I went to talk to the strikers. At the same time I reminded the management that I was not an agitator but was concerned about the shoe trade which I wanted to remain in New York. I told the workers the same thing and urged them to settle the strike immediately. I also told them I was not one to decry all management as thieves, praising my own employer as a decent man. This was a sharp contrast with the Communists who saw no good manufacturers.

I then proposed to Martin Weinstein that the issue could be resolved in one hour by convening the men in a hall where he could explain to them the benefits of remaining with the manufacturers group, while I would follow with a word about the benefits of joining the craft — AFL union. After the speeches the workers would vote by moving to one side of the room or the other depending on which union they preferred. As it turned out, I spoke first reminding the workers that they had engaged in a wildcat strike and were liable because they had broken a contract, although management was not calling for their arrest. Now, they wanted to become members of the AFL. I told them that we were open for new members and that by joining us they would not be isolated. At the same time, I told them they ought not expect the AFL to negotiate a new contract covering prices, that is, they were bound to carry out their old contract and not expect us to ignore it. When a new contract was due, we could work for an adjustment in prices. I asked each group of workers, the cutters, the fitters, the shoemakers, the lasters, the heelers, all of them as individual segments if they agreed to the proposal. The vote was set. Those who wanted to go with the AFL would move to the right of the room, while those who agreed to remain with the Board of Trade would move to the left. The result was 27 stayed on the left while 425 stood on the right. I shook hands, walked out of the place and expressed my best wishes. Afterwards, Martin Weinstein called my employer to tell him how impressed he was with me. He paid me the compliment of saying that I was born with an awl in my hand — a born shoemaker. "He feels for the shoemaker."

At that time our union had over 25,000 shoemakers in the Brooklyn area. Out of that number probably about 15,000 were Italian, about 20 percent were Jewish and the rest were mixed nationalities. Unfortunately, with the NRA and its limitation on income for the trade, the shoemakers lost a great deal. Most of them made less than they were getting before Roosevelt came in, as a price of thirty-seven and one-half cents per hour was set as the limit. Manufacturers took the view that if you made more than that you had no gripe because it was beyond the federal code. After this there was no future in the line. Roosevelt had killed the craft in Brooklyn.

Either Roosevelt was misled or did not care for the Italians in the trade, but he still had no right to mention the hourly wage of any skilled worker when he did not know the skills he was talking about. He never did consult with the workers in the trade and he finally disrupted a trade that was well established. Much of the shoemaking trade left this area at that time, much of it moving to other countries, where it has remained.

Remigio d. Pane

I was born in February, 1912, in Scigliano, a small village in the province of Cosenza, in southern Italy, located about 2,200 feet above sea level in the mountains of Calabria. My father, who had learned the shoemaking trade as a young man of 17, had been to America twelve years before I was born. Like other immigrants, during the early period of mass immigration to America, he did not know where to go upon arrival, so he went to the mining town of Dunmore, Pennsylvania, where a group of immigrants from his village had settled. Instead of shoemaking he joined the mine gangs as a brakeman on the cars that carried the coal from the mines to the outside. He was young and agile enough to sit on top of the car which had a crudely made brake consisting of a baseball bat which he put between the wheel and the rail. It worked for a couple of years until one day the bat broke and a piece of wood split his jaw. That was the end of mining for him and he left Dunmore and moved to Trenton, New Jersey, where he found a job shoemaking and where he remained until 1909. After he had earned a couple of hundred dollars, he returned to southern Italy and married. From that union, my sister was born in 1910 and I in 1912.

When I was seven months old he again migrated to America by himself since he knew he could make better money there than in Italy. This time he remained until the end of World War I, when he returned to Italy with the machinery to start a shoe repair shop, asserting that he had come back for good. In the meantime I had finished grammar school in Italy and had entered the *quinta elementare*. I was happy to see him return, of course, but then he read in the newspapers that emigration was going to come to a close and he had not yet become a citizen. Much as all the other immigrants who had come to the United States temporarily, he did not think it was necessary to become an American citizen. Now, however, when he read of the imminent close of immigration to the United States he told my mother he would have to return to America. He told her to bring the machines down to the cellar and oil them and he would be in touch with her. He left home that same day. A few days later we received a letter saying that he had booked passage for America and that we would be hearing from him. We did not hear from him for two months. It seemed he had found passage on a boat that was transporting wheat and it took him forty days to make the crossing. This time, however, the first thing he did was to become a citizen, and then he returned to Italy again in 1927.

By now I was 15 years old and I had finished elementary school, some grades in the *gymnasio* and I learned the trade of shoemaking. One evening I told my father that I would like to go to America. He agreed and I wrote the U.S. Consul in Naples who approved of my application since my father was a citizen. I then wrote to an uncle who was in the United States and asked him to send me a paid boat ticket which cost $198.00 gold dollars at that time. I was to go second class because my father thought it would be wiser since I was young. We went to Naples and arrived at the American Consulate where I was told that I could not go since I was not yet 18, unless I had an older relative to accompany me. My father decided quickly and said he would go but that he needed a little time to settle matters. We went back to town and he promised my mother that he would stay only long enough to earn travel expenses. This time he kept his word. In April, 1929 we landed in New York at Ellis Island where they gave me a green card as a permanent resident and I derived citizenship through my father. My father stayed for about a year and a half before he returned to Italy. I remained in Trenton where I had taken the job as shoemaker my father had had when he left.

I worked in this shop and started to go to "Americanization classes" in the evenings. I attended the old school Junior High No. 1 where my name became a problem. According to the English teacher there was no English equivalent for "Remigio". In the dictionary I found "Remy" which was the equivalent coming from the French. The teacher rejected the explanation saying it still did not sound "American". "We shall call you Raymond." I objected but could not explain myself in English and they could not understand Italian, so Raymond it became. That kind of thing occurred frequently to immigrants. The teacher was an excellent teacher but she wanted to assign American-sounding names. Pane (Pa-neigh) became "Pain". She worked hard with us and we learned some English. When the class ended in January she informed me of another evening school where they had a regular 8th grade class, knowing that I was interested in continuing. With her recommendation I went to the John Skelton School in South Trenton where they were doing 8th grade work, in an organized program which differed from the Americanization program. The teacher was a marvelous person with long experience in dealing with adults and foreigners and while the class did the regular work, she would join me in the back row and help me to write sentences. When she corrected my sentences there was more red ink than black, but she helped me immensely. Between January and May when the course finished I was able to pass the 8th grade examination. She wrote me a great letter of recommendation for me to attend the Trenton Accredited Evening High School.

In those days New Jersey had four accredited evening high schools and one of them, to my luck, happened to be in Trenton. The following fall I entered the Trenton Accredited Evening High School in the 9th grade. The school had the regular four year program, the only exception from the curriculum being that there was no physical education. During the day I worked in the shoemaker shop and at night attended four classes. This was during the depression in 1931. By 1933 we had to work longer hours in the shoe shop to keep our jobs. Wages had been reduced and instead of the $30.00 a week which I had been earning, I was down to $18.00, while the hours had been increased to almost 70 a week. We went to work in the early morning and I left at 6:00 p.m., insisting that I must go to school. On Saturdays, however, I worked until my work was finished which sometimes was 11:00 at night. Because of these conditions several workers and I organized a union which we called the Journeymen Shoebuilders Union of Mercer County. All of us who were wage earners joined and we demanded that the hours be reduced from 70 to 48. Although it was a modest request the owners objected. Finally under the threat of a strike they agreed. The owners got back at us by keeping within the 48 hours but staggering the hours in such a way that it made life unpleasant.

I became secretary of the union which included a good number of Italian Americans but not exclusively. One of the persons most interested in this and whom I was glad to help was a Jewish man who had a family and several children. In my case it did not make much difference because I was planning to leave to go to college which I soon did.

The neighborhood in which I lived in Trenton was only partially Italian. We lived near the Reading Railroad track where we rented a room from an Italian family. It was a boarding house among a number of row houses which had mixed nationalities. There was, however, in Trenton an Italian neighborhood, known as Chambersburg and it had an Italian parish which I attend. The clergy there were Italian and there were Italian sisters teaching Italian in the Catholic school which they continued until World War II.

In 1935, I graduated from the evening high school and was accepted at Rutgers University in New Brunswick where I started school in the Fall of 1935. I arranged my classes in the morning and went back to work in the shop in the afternoons and on Saturdays. At the end of the first semester, the shop in which I was working was sold as part of an estate. Being out of work and having to move to New Brunswick, I went to the Dean of Students at the college.

Before I went to Rutgers some people had advised me against going there since it had been started by the Dutch Reformed Church in America, and there was an assumption among my friends in Trenton that the school was prejudiced against Catholics. Deciding to take my chances, I knew the real test would come as I now went to see the Dean of Students who was a Dutch Reformed minister and school chaplain. I asked him if he knew of any faculty member who would agree to give a room to a student in exchange for services such as helping maintain the lawn, shoveling snow and the like. After he asked me several questions he picked up the phone and called someone by the name of Jessie to whom he later sent me. He told her to give me two sheets, pillow cases, etc., and the room on the right, downstairs. I was excited, of course, but I had no idea who Jessie was until I got to the house and found out she was Mrs. Metzger, his wife. He had agreed to give me a room in his own house. For the next three years I lived there taking care of the grounds, shoveling the snow and such.

Living at the Metzger house was a great opportunity for me. For example, some days the Dean entertained the speakers of the chapel. Whenever there was a speaker with extensive literary interest, Mrs. Metgzer invited me to dinner. In this way I was able to meet and enjoy the company of many interesting people such as Norman Thomas, who was a regular speaker at the Rutgers Chapel, and a personal friend of the Metzgers. Every time he came I was invited to dinner. There would usually be the four of us, Mr. and Mrs. Metzger, Norman Thomas, and I. It was a special opportunity for me, especially since Norman Thomas would recall his experiences working with the Italian immigrants in New York City and he took an interest in me.

During this time at the Metzgers I also kept my job in the shoemaker's shop in New Brunswick which I had obtained after losing the previous one. So, for my first two years at Rutgers, I took classes in the mornings and worked in the afternoons to pay for my tuition and food. I also received a small scholarship of $100.00 a year from the university. At the end of two years I had to make a choice. The owner of the shop in which I worked wanted to open another shop in another state and he offered me a full-time job as manager of the New Brunswick shoe repair shop. To take the job I would have had to quit college. This was in 1937 at the height of the depression. To discourage him I told him he could not afford to pay me what I wanted. He asked me to tell him what I wanted. I said $125.00 a week. He said all right, let's go to the lawyer and make a contract, "for five years". It was difficult for me to decide because the professors were not making that much money then; the Chairman of the Foreign Language Department was making only $3,500.00 a year. As manager of the shoe repair shop I would have made well over $5,000.00. So I went home and discussed the matter with the Dean. He was a little upset about this and asked me not to make any decisions until he spoke with me again. The next morning I had gone to work early when the Dean called me at the shop and told me that the State Legislature had just passed a scholarship aid program offering full tuition state scholarships and that if I remained at Rutgers, because of my record, he would be able to offer me such a scholarship. That was the straw that broke the camel's back. I told the shop owner that I would not accept his offer. He said to me that as a professor I would never make that much money, and, in those days, perhaps he was right. However, I never regretted it. I went back and to make good on the Dean's faith I doubled up my work and was able to finish in three years instead of four. I graduated in 1938 and in one more year I received my Master's degree. That same year Rutgers hired me as an instructor in romance languages and gave me a mandate to develop the Italian program which, modestly, I proceeded to do.

When World War II began I was still single. My family remained in Italy and I had been in regular contact with them sending the Sunday edition of the *New York Times* to my father. When the war started he wrote to me asking me not to send it anymore because he did not want to get into trouble. I considered myself an American citizen, and had registered to vote in Trenton when I became 21. I also had my green entrance card and my father's citizenship paper. I had tried to become a citizen at one point, by going to the federal court in Trenton before a judge who was one of my customers in the shoe shop and he said he could not make me a citizen twice. Later, I discovered that I could obtain my own derivative certificate which I applied for. Yet, because Italy became an enemy country during the war that certificate never came. The naturalization process was turned over to the Justice Department during World War II and every time I wrote a letter I received no answer. This worried me because I wanted to have a paper for my own security. In 1941 I had married a girl of Italian background who was born in this country but I still did not have the papers. Finally, in 1942 a newspaper clipping from Trenton was sent to me by a friend which listed my father among a group whose citizenship was terminated. Apparently when I had made my request for papers the clerk who did the investigation checked and found that my father had left the United States four years after receiving papers. The clerk had not really made a thorough investigation because she overlooked the fact that my father had returned with me in 1929. Immediately I petitioned the court to allow me to be a co-defendant. Eventually the case was dismissed, and in 1944 I finally received my own citizenship paper.

I know of no other Italian Americans in the New Brunswick area who suffered discrimination during the war. They were loyal Americans and supported the war. During the war over 1,000 Italian prisoners were stationed at the Raritan Arsenal. Under an international agreement prisoners were allowed to work in the arsenal and paid $1.00 a day. After I contacted the authorities, the thirty-six United States Army lieutenants who had just finished the Army Specialized Training Program in Italian at Rutgers, were assigned to work with these prisoners because they could use the language in their work immediately. I also worked out and conducted a program to teach the prisoners English. I taught these 40 Italian officers, headed by an infantry colonel from Sicily. The Americans were rather judicious I think because they treated these men humanely and the arsenal was open for visiting. Thousands of Italo-Americans flocked there from all over the country because among these prisoners, there were many relatives of American citizens. I remember one Sunday while walking with the Italian colonel, a small Italo-American came over to the colonel and tried to kiss his hand. The colonel froze and withdrew his hand and embraced the man instead. It turned out that this elderly man had worked for the colonel's family while he was a young boy in Italy. The elderly Italian remembered the old Italian habits even though he was in America. The colonel, to his credit, did not accept the old-time fealty.

Some of these prisoners married the local girls. In 1938, while I was finishing my MA degree, I needed some support. I got a job with the WPA to teach evening school after convincing a principal that there were people who would want to study Italian. The following Monday night, much to the principal's surprise, there were about 60 people ready to sign up for the course. One of those who registered became a bride of an Italian prisoner of war. After the war she went to Sicily, married him and both came over here. They now have four children, all of whom graduated from college.

Incidentally, after a few weeks, the authorities agreed to allow the prisoners out on leave on Sundays with the local Italian people. Some local people came and invited some of the prisoners over for a Sunday meal. The local non-Italian people did not generally resent this, but there were a few instances, which were exceptions. I remember one newspaper editorial which sought to "remind" people that these prisoners were our enemies. There were also letters to the editors, from people who had lost sons in the service, which expressed their displeasure at this fraternization. As a result of the furor these letters produced, the military authorities suspended the Sunday passes for prisoners until the uproar abated. Gradually, there was less and less opposition. When Italy later joined the Allies, the local Italo-American population was accepted by the community.

The men who were in my special Italian language program at Rutgers were not all Italo-Americans since they included a good number of people chosen by the army as a result of aptitude tests. All of them were college graduates and several were already school teachers. They were candidates for officers school and underwent an intensive training which included not only language but history and other courses. We were preparing other students in other languages, i.e., French, Spanish, etc., in what was one of the first pilot programs in intensive language training in the country. At one point I tried to bring in Carlo Sforza to explain something about Italian history, but I was unable to obtain him since he had agreed to lecture at another school.

About this time, there was one occurence with the famous Italian born professor at Columbia, Giuseppe Prezzolini. From 1939 to 1941, while I was teaching at Rutgers, I took courses with Professor Prezzolini who was then director of Casa Italiana. I have remained friends with him over the years. Some years ago, when I was in Italy, he was being honored on his ninetieth birthday, with a book in which a number of his formers students were asked to comment on his influence as a teacher. I was glad to contribute to this work because he was a professor who prepared for his classes whether they were large or small and we all received specific and individual attention. I saw no evidence in any of his classes of proselytizing on any political ideas. I even took a course on Macchiavelli with Professor Prezzolini where the opportunity for political propaganda exists, but there was not a trace of fascism. In all the classes with him and others, there simply were no politics. I remember one Sunday evening when Walter Winchell, who was the prime gossiper of the United States, announced, as if he were discovering the North Pole, that there was a fascist at Columbia University — Professor Prezzolini of Casa Italiana. Everyone knew that before coming to the United States Professor Prezzolini had been a journalist in Italy and in Paris and that he had written articles on fascism, on Mussolini, recognizing in 1924, that Mussolini was going to be an important figure in Italy. Immediately following Winchell's broadcast Prezzolini resigned as director of Casa Italiana, although he remained as a professor of Italian. A number of us went to him and expressed our wishes that he continue to teach and continue to build the Paterno Library over which he presided. In his cordial way he assured us that he would remain as professor but that it would be best for the institution if he resigned as director. Knowing the uprightness of this man, a number of us reasoned that his decision was probably correct since Italy was an enemy nation. We spontaneously decided to give the professor a gift, chipping in some money to buy him a short-wave radio set. When the two students gave it to Professor Prezzolini he accepted the card that went with it but refused the radio. I still have the personal letter he sent to all of us thanking us for the thought. He felt like a professor should not accept gifts from students.

I did not get involved with Italian organizations like the Sons of Italy. Perhaps I am the exception among Italian Americans. When I came from Italy, I lived in an Italian ambience in Trenton; I went to the Italian Church; and I worked with an uncle who spoke Italian and I realized that I was not learning any English. I remember once when I got a job with an Irishman, I would bring my lunch in my brown bag and I would bring it back home at night because I did not understand what he was saying when he said I could have lunch. Consequently, I began to frequent English-speaking neighborhoods and I did not join any organizations at all. I never really had time between working and going to school. When I was in college I felt it was my job to teach Italian and develop the program and that was a full time job. I am happy I concentrated on it and did not become embroiled in groups which became factionalized over politics.

during the fascist era. I did belong, however, to all the language associations in the country and now I am also a member of the American Italian Historical Association. I always respected other groups but I felt that in an academic position I would do best by keeping with academic associations. Over the years I have been a speaker at Italian American organizations as well as professional organizations. I speak at least thirty to forty times a year on Italian culture and, lately, on the Italian American experience.

Prior to my development of the Italian language program at Rutgers, there was not much of an offering in Italian although the course was in the catalogue and was open to seniors. The chairman of the department who was a French professor occasionally offered a course, but it was reserved for juniors and seniors who could only take a maximum of two years. By 1935, when I entered Rutgers, there was a strong Italian Club that had been chartered in 1932. I collaborated with the club and by 1938, when I graduated, the club had petitioned for a class in Italian and had recommended me to teach it. The department went along except for the chairman, who felt that anyone who was born abroad should not be hired as a full-time instructor. It was not because he was prejudiced against Italians, but because he felt from his experience, it would be better to have only American born teachers. Because of the encouragement from the rest of the department, however, I remained at Rutgers, and the following year when I received my Masters, the chairman retired, and the department hired me.

My teaching career at Rutgers began in 1939 when I taught Spanish and started courses in Italian. When the war came, languages all but disappeared. Yet, in 1943 the first Italian major graduated Rutgers — a student who later went abroad and became assistant to Governor Poletti when Poletti was administrator of Italy. Another student who majored in Italian with me also performed well in the service in Italy during the war. After the war, when the veterans came back and Italian flourished, I stayed with the university receiving promotions until I became a full professor. In 1952 my colleagues elected me chairman of the Department of Romance Languages, a position in which I served for 19 years, until 1971. During this period of expansion of foreign languages the department expanded from nine full-time teachers in 1952 to forty-three in 1971 along with twenty-eight teaching assistants. In Italian alone we had six full professors with a staff of eleven. I stepped down in 1971, desiring to spend the last five or six years teaching and spending time in the library rather than in administrative duties. The departments were then divided into the three departments of Spanish/Portugese, French, and Italian. We reached the point where we had one hundred Ph.D. candidates in Italian. The majority of our students in the Italian program are of Italian background but there are a considerable number of people studying the language with non-Italian names. From the beginning it was my policy that if Italian was any good it was also worthwhile for others to study it. If French depended only upon students with a French background they would never have enough students. I think the old policy of trying to encourage students of Italian background to study Italian was counterproductive, especially with the first generation of Italian Americans who had experienced discrimination or who had not known English because their parents had spoken Italian at home. Now with the third and fourth generation of Italian Americans and after the Second World War when Americans found that Italy was not what they had thought it was, there was a sort of natural desire to know about Italy and Italians.

The reluctance to study Italian on the part of the first generation was indeed due to a sense of discrimination. I remember when I was first hired as an instructor that during freshman registration many students would freeze when they saw "Italian" and would move towards Spanish, French and other languages. The chairman of the department, who was anxious to develop the Italian course, would see students with Italian names and express his surprise at the way they would avoid taking the language. The young men would hardly be able to respond. Eventually, after speaking to a number of these students, I found the problem was simple. Parents who had come over from Italy and who had not had the opportunity to go to school did not know how to read or write Italian. Here, they were not helped to learn English. Consequently, their children learned the dialect of their parents and when they went into the streets to play with other children, they did not understand each other. These children were foreigners in America although born here. In elementary school they dressed differently, they spoke different languages and they brought different lunches to school. They felt bad and they attributed it to their background. This, of course, created psychological problems at home and at school. When these children grew up they went to high school where Italian still was not taught, so they did not have to face that problem. When they came to college, however, and saw Italian, naturally they shied away. Now when their children in turn came along they brought up their children to speak English. The Americanization programs and World War II also served to accent this problem.

I do not think I experienced any discrimination myself or, if there were any I did not notice it. Rev. Metzger and the rest of the people at Rutgers treated me excellently. At the same time, I do not know whether there were any other Italian Americans on the Rutgers faculty. I am not sure whether this can be attributed to discrimination or to the fact that there were not enough candidates. College graduates of Italian background were, until very recently, not abundant. The early graduates usually went into the profession that their parents knew in the villages, the doctor, lawyer and the pharmacist or the school teacher, but not necessarily as college professors.

Our language department at Rutgers is largely a literature department, but I had proposed two years ago that a course on the Italian American experience be offered since the history department did not offer one. The course was approved by the department and the faculty and I have taught it, learning a great deal in the process. It has been a very satisfying experience. Most of the students are of Italian background but we also pulled in others. The great thing about this course was that it opened my eyes to a new problem. Richard Gambino, toward the end of his book *Blood of My Blood,* says that this problem that the third and fourth generation Italian Americans are facing is the crisis of identity. Am I Italian or am I American? What does it mean to be an "Italian or an American?" Well, it would seem that he is right on this point. Several of the students in the class came since they were attracted by the title. We read Rolle's book and Tomasi and Engle's book, then Amphitheatrof's and finally Gambino's book which I felt was a kind of psychological inside examination, which should come later. Some of the students found that what they needed was this identity which was some sort of self-finding. I required each one of them to do a research paper on a family, not necessarily their own, which had at least three generations in America. Most of them did their own and they learned a great deal. One girl admitted that she had not spoken to her grandmother for a long time because she thought her grandmother was not up to her level since she was going to college. Well, she spent several weekends interviewing her grandmother and came away with a completely new appreciation. The girl now considers her grandmother the most intelligent member of the whole family. The student herself, gained a new sense of self-respect which she did not have before. I find in this a great sense of satisfaction. I should like to see an increase of these courses not only in college but at other levels and at a recent meeting of the New Jersey language teachers I suggested this. I think we can do much to help Italian American students study their background and be proud rather than ashamed. With this new-found level of self-respect they will be able to achieve better work in their other subjects and thereby help counter the perennial problem of the Italian

American dropout.

I feel that my experience from 1929 to the present has been a rich experience made possible by the local condition and by my own personal contributions. The elements are here as, in fertile ground, but unless you plant the seed and cultivate it, it will not grow. I hope my fellow Italo-Americans will realize the fertility of the ground and will contribute by plowing, seeding, and fertilizing so their own harvest may be as rich as mine has been.

~ THREE ~

The Poet
and
The Artist

Introduction

Universally acknowledged for their literary and artistic achievements in Italy, the Italian contribution to the arts became far less conspicuous in the American setting. In fact, Americans were much more likely to associate Italian immigrants with the strenuous, unskilled labor which did, in truth, describe the greater portion of immigrant employment. This economic backdrop notwithstanding, there were Italian immigrants whose passion for literature and art was so strong that they made it their lifetime work; often at great expense to themselves and to their families. For those who chose literature and art as their vocation, earning a livelihood would not be easy. In their fellow Italians they were confronted with an immigrant population which came from a pre-modern society which had little use for scholarly learning.

Each of the men whose autobiographies follow was from different Italian sub-cultures and different time periods. The first to present his story, Joseph Zappulla, was born in 1901 in the mountain region of eastern Sicily and migrated to the United States in 1919. At the time of my meeting with him he was a senior citizen whose career was largely behind him. The second story included here is that of Giovanni Pinna who was born in the pastoral setting of Sardinia and came to this country in 1963; his career is largely ahead of him.

Barely five feet tall, Joseph Zappulla, was a giant in Italian American letters. His love of the written word in the Italian language was such that few gifted writers and poets of Italian ancestry in America could match. Few labored so long and as lonely and equally few approached his poetic sensibilities as he recorded in verse his thoughts and feelings, always aware of his Sicilian roots. Because he wrote primarily in Italian he has received only limited acclaim for his poetry in the United States.

I first met Joseph Zappulla in the winter of 1976 in Patchogue, New York, where he lived in a pleasant apartment with his wife, Rita. I maintained contact with him for the next year and a half, until his death in the summer of 1977. Born in Siracusa, Sicily, in 1901 and armed with a limited formal education, he emigrated to the United States while a young man and became a self-taught man of letters — a rarity in the American society. Over the course of a half century of professional life he followed an intense and varied journalistic career writing hundreds of articles on many subjects which appeared in almost all the major Italian language publications in the United States. He wrote plays, short stories, essays and adaptations for the Italian radio in America, serving also on various stations as a lecturer and news commentator. During World War II he was a script editor for the Voice of America and the Columbia Broadcasting System. In addition, he published his own Italian American newspaper and literary journals. His crowning achievement, however, was his poetry acclaimed by some of the most noted critics as among the finest poetry of his time.

Mario Pei, foremost linguist and critic, openly admired Zappulla's poetry:

[it demonstrates a] purity of form, clarity of ideas, and absolute mastery of the Italian language. The gossamer-like delicacy of many of his concepts; the exquisiteness of his feelings, and his handling of images and figures of speech [sic]. Here is a man who writes in the noble tradition of Alfieri and Foscolo, of Leopardi and Carducci, a man who doesn't give up the struggle and resign himself to obscure language.

A Milan newspaper, Il Caminetto, *wrote that his poetry is "One of the most perfect, one of the highest and most human voices of modern Italian poetry". His published works of poetry* "Voci nell'ombra, Vette ed Abissi", *(1936).* "Poesie", *(1956) and* "Mete Lontane", *(1962) were written in Italian and published in Italy.*

Giovanni Pinna earns his livelihood as an artist, designing and working plastic fibers into sculpture. He not only makes his own works but also teaches this form of art to others and has enjoyed some degree of success in the medium. His vocation as an artist is a recent development, since he had previously earned his living working in a variety of unskilled jobs. Both of his grandfathers helped build the Panama Canal and both mined the coal fields of Pennsylvania, yet he was born and raised in Sardinia, coming to this country in 1963 at the age of eighteen. He served as a United States soldier in the Vietnam War and has proceeded to embark upon a college career.

It was while he was a student at Nassau Community College that I first met Giovanni Pinna, then calling himself John. He was a student in my class, "History of American Immigrant/Ethnic Groups", and provided effective and meaningful examples of what recent immigrants must undergo before they can gain acceptance in this country's contemporary social setting. Moreover, as a Sardinian who savored strongly the pastoral society of the Italian island of Sardinia and as a keen observer of contemporary American society, he is in a position to comment intelligently about both cultures. As such he extends to us additional insight into the ongoing experience of the odyssey from immigration to Americanization.

W hen I left my native town in Eastern Sicily at the age of nineteen to come to America, "the Promised Land", I fully expected to return for at least a short visit, within a few years.

My father was a mason; house builder and repairer in a small agricultural town of fewer than 5,000 inhabitants where his trade offered him little more than enough to feed and clothe his family. He had five children of whom I was the third. When he died, at 48, a victim of pneumonia, I was only sixteen years old and because my brother, the first born, was studying for the priesthood in another town and wished to continue his studies, the responsibility of taking care of my mother and my three sisters fell upon my shoulders. It was a painful and hard task. No matter how I struggled I never seemed to earn enough even for the basic needs. My brother managed to continue his studies through what help he was given by the church, which I cannot remember. My sisters never married.

The thought of coming to the United States where I had some relatives occurred to me immediately after my father's death in the spring of 1917. First, however, I had to wait for the end of the war. Then, I had to wait to obtain a passport, and I waited again to find passage. It was almost the end of 1920 before I was finally able to leave. During those long years before my departure I spent the money my relatives had sent me for the voyage and I had to ask for more money. It took me several years in the United States before I managed to extinguish this debt.

Long before my father's death I had felt a great desire to go away. I had always dreamed of living in the city, any city, not only because whenever I had visited even a larger town than my own I had been fascinated, but also because I had been an avid reader since childhood and my imagination had been fired by the accounts of voyages, adventures and enjoyments I had read. My native town had seemed to me a jail from which I had an irresistable compulsion to escape. It was situated at an altitude of 2,690 feet, but it was surrounded by hills on every side and I felt closed-in, watched, and materially impeded in my wish to flee. From the tops of those hills, on clear days, I could see a great expanse of country, several towns breaking the green of the plains; majestic Mount Aetna in the far distance; the city of Catania spread out at its base; and, at times, even the sea dotted with white sails and the coast of Calabria. All this gave wings to my desire to go away and often I was on the verge of running away without knowing or caring where I went.

When I arrived in New York, in 1922, and went to live in the Little Italy, whose center was Mulberry Street, I was pleasantly surprised to see the many Italian newspapers and magazines published in the city that was then considered "the biggest Italian city" after Naples.

Naples itself, with its 800,000 inhabitants, seemed even to have transplanted many of its popular quarters to this section of New York where everything was Italian although not exclusively Neapolitan: the people crowding the streets; the cafes; the restaurants; the stores; the music issuing from the stores that sold phonographs and records; and the vendor carts along the sidewalks. In the afternoon there were even newsboys screaming the headlines of an afternoon daily paper called *Bollettino della Sera.* The headlines of the day could also be seen on the newpapers, printed in red ink across the front page.

There were two other daily papers called *Il Progresso Italo-Americano,* and the *Corriere d'America.* On Mulberry Street a large book store, the Italian Book Company, sold Italian books of all kinds and religious images and articles. Nearby was a cubicle where I found a weekly newspaper entitled *La Follia di New York,* and a monthly magazine entitled *Il Carroccio.* There was also a weekly illustrated magazine, *La Domenica Illustrata,* with which I was already familiar. Before arriving in New York I had been "shipped" to a city near Boston, Massachusetts, where I had relatives. There, I had first found *La Domenica* which later published some of my early poems. Because *La Follia* published many poems and asked for contributions, I began to send it other poems and, later, articles. At the time, of course, I was not mature enough to judge poetry with a positive sureness but it did not take me long to realize that *La Follia* published much worthless stuff, thereby encouraging and praising a great number of illiterate individuals who should have been discouraged. It often published a whole page of poems — in the various Italian dialects — whose authors could not even write a letter in Italian without making one error after another. Most of these "poets" wrote only to satisfy their vanity. It was an easy way to appear superior to their *paesani*. Others wanted to express genuine nostalgia for their native towns as well as other sentiments, but they still were not poets and had no skill at all. *La Follia* profited by this outpouring of so-called poetry because every contributor not only became a subscriber, but also procured subscriptions, and bought many copies. All this, I thought, was detrimental to art and literature. The bad example set by *La Follia* had already been imitated by many other Italian publications all over the country. Later this same 'hospitality' was also offered by publications which, up to then, had not accepted poetry of any kind.

Il Progresso Italo-Americano is the oldest Italian daily published in the United States, and perhaps the only one still surviving. Most of the other dailies had ceased publishing by 1922. Whatever its shortcomings the Italian press in America performed a useful function. Without these publications (or at least many of them) the Italian immigrants would have suffered much more than they did. One of the principal handicaps of immigrants is their ignorance of the language of the host country. Italian immigrants were able then to turn to the publications printed in their own language, for information and guidance. It was through newspapers that they found an apartment or a furnished room, a restaurant, a bank, and often a job. The press made them feel less isolated and less bewildered, while furnishing them with a variety of information and news from Italy (although for many immigrants Italy meant only their native town or province). The press induced the immigrants to read, many of whom had never or rarely read a newspaper. The papers in their native towns also informed them about what was happening to other Italian immigrants, and furnished them with information about the Italian associations, the various banquets, feasts, churches and politicians.

The *Corriere d'America* was founded shortly before my arrival in New York by the Milanese industrialist Pio Crespi, who owned a cotton plantation in Texas (as I was told when I went to work for the paper, without ever having investigated this information). The editor was a famous journalist, Luigi Barzini, who later returned to Italy and became the editor of *Il Mattino* of Naples. The *Corriere* was not much better than *Il Progresso,* since many members of the editorial staff did not write or translate well and were unable to condense the news furnished by the United Press. Barzini's editorials, however, were eagerly read and appreciated. I joined the staff around 1930 and since I had already written a good deal for other newspapers and magazines, I was asked to contribute to its Sunday Literary Supplement, which I did without compensation, as did two other members of the staff: Augusto Nauro and Franco Lalli, both of whom were good writers. Most of the pieces were simply taken from newspapers and magazines we received from Italy. My stay with the *Corriere* was short, although I was called back years later when Mussolini declared war on the United States. A few members of the staff at that time, in their admiration for Mussolini and Hitler, had naively exalted and pledged their loyalty to Fascism and had been interned. With the war on, however, this and other publications lost the advertisements of the Italian shipping companies, banks, importers, etc., and Generoso Pope, who had bought the paper after having bought many other dailies (plus one in Philadelphia, Pa., entitled *L'Opinione*) closed the *Corriere* down. A short time later I went to work for the Office of War Information.

Il Carroccio, a good monthly magazine which had supported facism and had quarreled with its Foreign Minister Dino Grandi, was forced to close down. I had contributed very little to it with an occasional poem and a non-political article (I never wrote about politics). *Il Carroccio* dedicated its August issue each year to literature and most of its content was quite good including the local contributions. I had a few laughs at its expense once when it published some poems by the Canadian Protestant Minister Liborio Lattoni. They seemed nothing less than parodies of Carducci's *Odi Barbare.* Lattoni, however, had not intended them as parodies. He simply could not write differently and because of their patriotic tone the magazine's publisher and editor Agostino De Biasi (a good polemist) published them not realizing that they were laughable.

Three other good monthly magazines were *Columbus, Atlantica* and *Vittoriale.* The first lasted longest of the three because its publisher and editor, Campora, owned a printing shop. The second was created for idealistic reasons by a physician, Dr. Cassola. *Vittoriale* was published by Giovanni Favoino di Giura who had previously published a book of his war memories entitled *Trincea.* He was, like De Biasi, an admirer of Mussolini but when he asked me to contribute to his magazine, I obliged and ignored the political considerations since I was writing only about literature.

About that time there were two other Italian dailies in New York *Il Nuovo Mondo* and *La Stampa Libera,* both of which were antifascist. *Il*

Nuovo Mondo had been founded earlier, but because of dissension among the people who supported it, some members of the staff, headed by Girolamo Valenti, left and began to publish *La Stampa Libera.*

Fascism had some rabid supporters until their idol declared war on the United States. The most violent newspaper, a weekly entitled *Il Grido della Stirpe,* was published by Domenico Trombetta who once criticized Barzini for not being too enthusiastic about fascism in *Corriere d'America.* A monthly magazine of the same stripe was entitled *Giovinezza.* Its editor, a young fanatic, imitated Mussolini's style and even the handwriting. Gradually, many Italian publications of all kinds disappeared. In Chicago there was a daily called *L'Italia,* but I never saw it. Another daily with the same title was published in San Francisco. This one I knew mainly because a New York journalist, Paolo Pallavicini-Pirovano, who had written two or three popular novels, had gone to work there. The paper folded soon after it published an article of mine, although I'm sure there was no connection between the two events. Another daily, *La Notizia,* was published in Boston.

There were several weekly papers besides *La Follia. Il Martello,* published by the anarchist Carlo Tresca who was killed in 1942 or 1943, was an interesting paper. Another leftist paper was *Il Proletario.* Many newspapers were also published by people who had no political, idealistic or humanitarian aims but who merely wanted to make a living in journalism. Whether qualified or not they barely succeeded. In New York there were *Il Nuovo Vessillo, Il Corriere del Bronx* and others. They never published anything really interesting and specialized in small family events. One well-written one was the anarchist paper *L'Adunata dei Refrattari.*

Once, in 1929, I was called by a man who published a weekly newspaper in Yonkers, New York, entitled *Corriere dell' Hudson.* I worked there for a while, trying to make it as interesting as possible. Earlier, in 1927, I had been editor of *La Sicilia,* a weekly which two other men had wanted to publish. I had suggested a different title, because the name of one region would not appeal to readers from other regions (and later there were papers and magazines called *Corriere Siciliano, La Calabria* and *Risveglio Trentino),* but I gave in because I wanted to say things that I could not say without having a paper in which I was free to write as I pleased. In *La Sicilia* I wrote a series of articles pointing out the absolute absence of any literary merit of several books of poetry which other publications had trumpeted as great works of art. *La Sicilia* had a brief life.

Once I spent a couple of months in Detroit, where some people wanted to start a paper to rival two that were already being published. No agreement was reached and I returned to New York.

I also stayed for three or four months in Wilkes-Barre, Pennsylvania, where I was called to edit a newspaper published by someone who, of course, could not write but who wanted to make a living in the publishing field. The publisher of that paper had a printing shop, which was losing money, and a costly office. I never knew what the circulation of his paper was, but I am sure it was not large since most of the subscribers were illiterate coal miners. At one point the publisher was so short of means that he could not pay me. Finally, he managed to get some money, but I had decided to return to New York. While I was in Wilkes-Barre he took me to another town where he wanted to rent an office and establish another newspaper since he was good at getting advertisements. I decided against this, however, since I knew no one in either Wilkes-Barre or the other town and because he told me the title of the paper would be *L'Universo*. I simply could not see myself editing a newspaper for miners with a title suitable for a magazine on astronomy.

A New York friend told me years later that the publisher had gone to Wilkes-Barre to take my place and that the man did publish a newspaper of that title for some time. My friend told me of an amusing episode he had one day at press time when the printing press would not work. He struggled for hours to get it going and as soon as he had one copy printed the publisher told him to stop since he needed only one copy of the paper to show a store-owner who had given him a half-page ad!

While in Pennsylvania I visited a friend in Scranton who was publishing another weekly, called *Il Minatore*. His name was Ludovico Caminita and he had previously worked for *Il Bollettino della Sera*. He was a good writer and had written a book which I reviewed favorably. Later he published a book on the life of the Peanut King, Amedeo Obici, who, starting as a peanut vendor, had become a millionaire.

In 1938 I went to Boston to take the place of an ailing editor of the weekly *Gazzetta del Massachusetts*. The publisher, as usual, did not write, but was capable of getting advertisements. He had 'correspondents' in every town and village of the state and published all kinds of small news concerning the Italians. One day he gave me a letter sent to him by one of his correspondents whose only item consisted of the information that Mr. So and So had just sold one of his goats. I asked the publisher if he really wanted to publish that news and he said "of course!" I remained there only eight months.

While I was in Boston my friend Giovanni Nania asked me to help him put out a bimonthly newspaper. He had a half-hour radio program in Italian and thought he would easily obtain sufficient advertisements. I did help him, or rather, I put together the whole paper, which he called *Radiostampa.* After a few issues, however, we had to quit because the income did not cover the printing expense.

A few political exiles who had a hard time making a living in the United States tried to manage by publishing a magazine. A former member of the Italian parliament, Vincenzo Vacirca, tried twice: first with *Il Solco* and years later with *La Strada* (or vice versa). Both were monthly magazines and did not last long. The Italian immigrants simply did not support the Italian press. Another exile, Giuseppe Lupis, published *Il Mondo,* also a monthly and also well written. When the war ended he returned to Italy and became Minister of Tourism and, later, Minister of Merchant Marine.

A former attorney, Ernesto Valentini, published an excellent magazine strangely called *Zarathustra.* He did not realize that most of his readers had never read Nietzsche. It too was short lived. In 1936 we worked together on a WPA project on Ellis Island. He had written a good book, *Il Ricatto,* in defense of a physician, Nicola Brunori, who had been innocently involved in a shabby blackmail plot for which he had to spend some time in jail.

There were also several weekly magazines. The first, after *La Domenica Illustrata,* was *La Geria,* a popular magazine published by the printers, Cocce Bros. and edited by Franco Lalli, a good writer who later published a literary monthly called *Panorama* and wrote an excellent book on Columbus and other explorers entitled *L'Immortale Canaglia,* which was published in Florence by Vallecci.

Fiorello La Guardia (not yet Mayor of New York at this time) and others published a popular weekly called *L'Americolo* (an indefensible title). Another weekly magazine, *La Settimana,* came out later through the efforts of Andre Luotto, helped by Lalli. Despite its failure Luotto tried again years later with another magazine, wrongly called *Divagando.*

One reason none of these publications lasted long lay in the fact that the majority of the Italians in the United States did not read, and those who did preferred the daily papers. Also most of them were reluctant to spend money for subscriptions. The barber around the corner from my house in Brooklyn was a subscriber, but his friend the grocer, next door to him, was not. The barber, of course, would pass the magazine on to the grocer every week after reading it. The grocer, in turn, gave it to the butcher, and I presume that the butcher passed it on to someone else. So a single subscription was enough for four or five readers, all of whom had no idea of the cost involved in publishing a magazine.

Several newspapers and magazines I worked on were published with the certainty that they would not be financially profitable, but we persisted, always hoping that at least we could make enough to cover our costs, even if we could not put a dollar in our pockets. I published one magazine every month for over a year, in the fifties, just because there was no one saying the things I felt had to be said. I entitled it *Novità* (previously I had published a similar magazine for a short period called *Luce*). Eventually I had to give up forever. Other writers, before and after me, also had to give up the idea of publishing a literary magazine. One of them was Giovanni Schiavo, who had published the *Vigo Review*.

There were two satirical magazines: *Maschere,* which Franco Lalli and I had fun putting together: and *Vita* one of the rare publications that paid me regularly. Both were short-lived. Only once or twice I saw *Giustizia,* a journal dedicated to labor problems and published by Local 89 of the International Ladies Garment Workers Union whose manager was Luigi Antonini. It was edited by Vanni Montana.

Some publications were simply commercial enterprises, such as *Il Commerciante Italiano,* circulating among Italian grocers, and *Il Calzolaio,* made for the Italian shoe repairers. As usual, their publishers did not write but needed writers, whom they never paid adequately. I wrote for both of these publications — one a weekly paper and the other a monthly magazine. *Il Calzolaio* was published regularly despite the fact that most of those to whom it was sent did not read anything or had no time to read a trade publication. The publisher, who owned a factory that manufactured ink, glue and other things used in the shoe repair trade, knew that most of the Italian shoe repairers did not read the American magazine dedicated to the trade, which carried many pages of advertisements for machinery, leather, rubber heels, etc. He thought, then, to publish a similar one in Italian. He did obtain enough ads to make his venture (which lasted many years) worthwhile.

An organization created during the war, the Mazzini Society, published the weekly *Nazioni Unite* which ceased publication when the war ended.

Another weekly for which I wrote a couple of articles was called

L'Interprete. It was published by a Protestant minister in Newburgh, New York. Many years earlier, in 1923 or 1924, I had seen another publication edited by a Protestant minister. This one was called *L'Idea.* I had forgotten it and it came to mind many years later because I contributed to a Roman magazine entitled *Idea.*

There were, of course, many weekly newspapers published outside of New York which I never saw. There was one paper, however, entitled *La Tribuna Transatlantica,* which had the pecularity of being written in a mixture of Italian and Neapolitan dialect.

Another paper of which I saw a single copy was *La Stella,* from Roseto, Pennsylvania. It contained a canto of a fantastic poem imitating Ariosto's *Orlando Furioso,* with the difference that it contained not a single poetical line. Its author was a prolific versifier whose several books of verse were really made up of bad prose in verse form and who was convinced that anything becomes poetry when set in verse form. The most striking thing in that issue was a Latin poem in which the author complained that some people had not acknowledged his Christmas greetings!

A third paper of which I have seen only one copy was *Il Crociato,* a Catholic weekly edited by Carlo De Biasi, a brother of the editor of *Il Carroccio.*

One magazine worth reading is still published monthly in Chicago by Egidio Clemente, who runs a printing establishment. It is a socialist magazine which prints many articles on a variety of subjects, including literature, and several poems — some good and some less so. A special issue appeared in July—August 1974 with excellent translations by Professor Joseph Tusiani of two of Manzoni's poems.

The bilingual monthly *Italamerican,* was published over ten years, until 1964 or 1965 by Vittorio De Fiori, who had also written a book on Mussolini. Soon after I began to contribute to it, Di Fiori gave me free rein (nominating me as associate editor) and for nine years I published many articles and a page of commentary. I believe that I helped make it something worth reading and I was glad that the publisher followed my advice not to publish trash in either prose or verse. For a while its managing editor was Lando Landi, who had recently arrived from Italy. When *Italamerican* was sold it was transformed completely and Landi became editor of a new weekly paper called *Corriere di New York.* This paper was published by an Italian Canadian who owned other papers in Canada. It was a good paper. I was glad to write for it and I was fairly compensated. Yet, it did not last long. Landi disappeared after that, but in 1971 I saw him in Rome in the office of *Novella 2000,* a weekly magazine published by Rizzoli. He was then head of the magazine's Roman office where he is still employed.

Of course there were many other publications which I never saw and others which I have forgotten. In the course of over half a century I have contributed to many of the publications mentioned, in addition to the quarterly bulletin of the American Association of Teachers of Italian, *Italica,* one of the best Italian literary magazines in the United States. Now, the trend is to publish ethnic newspapers and magazines in English. In addition to *Italica* there is *Italian Quarterly* and *Forum Italicum.* There are also two monthly newspapers: The *National Italian-American News* published in Brooklyn, New York, and the *Italo-American Times* published in the Bronx. An excellent publication whose demise I regret was the *Cesare Barbieri Courier,* published twice a year by the Cesare Barbieri Center of Italian Studies at Trinity College, Hartford, Connecticut. It was edited by Professor Michael R. Campo.

During that time I also had some experience with Italian radio programs. When Giuseppe Sterni, one of the best Italian actors in the United States, established *Il Teatro d'Arte Italiano* I attended and reviewed his monthly performances at the Bijou Theatre. I appreciated his efforts to give the Italians a series of good theatre performances, with a company he had organized and trained himself. To realize his project he performed the heroic task of convincing a good number of wealthy Italians to subscribe in advance to a number of performances and, for a while, he was able to produce well known excellent plays, both Italian and foreign. Later we became friends. He admired my poetry so much that he often recited it on the radio and once or twice printed one of my poems in the playbill he had distributed in the theatre at each performance.

At the conclusion of his series of performances he was engaged by a macaroni manufacturing company to give plays, in daily episodes, over the Italian radio station WOV. Each play was adapted for the radio, with a reduced number of actors, to about 20 minute episodes. Often a play took more than thirty days to be broadcast in its entirety. It seems that the listeners enjoyed these bits of acting and never lost track of characters and events.

One day he came to see me at the *Corriere d'America* and asked me if I would adapt some plays for him for the radio. I agreed, although he could not offer me more than two dollars for each episode, which took four or five typewritten pages. For each episode he sketched in a few words, what such and such characters were to say, so that my task consisted, substantially, in diluting long speeches to a few sentences.

It was a new experience for me and in a sense I enjoyed it. Sometimes he gave me free rein, telling me only that the play had to last so many days. Once he gave me an old book narrating the story of the Leoncavallo's opera *I Pagliacci* which I sketched into 13 episodes. Naturally, I did this work at home in the evening and sent him my work by mail. After broadcasting such plays as *I Pagliacci,* Gerolamo Rovetta's *Romanticismo,* a French play entitled *Il Colonnello Bridau* and others he realized that these plays were too high-class for the masses and resorted to popular stories, one of which, *The Life of Saint Anthony,* he concocted in a way that left me bewildered for the strange and unlikely events that it narrated.

When my collaboration with Sterni came to an end I was asked by other heads of similar dramatic companies to write episodes for them. I remember one long series of episodes written from a popular (and absurd) novel by Carolina Invernizio, the most popular Italian novelist of all times, entitled *La Sepolta Viva.* This series was also being produced by another Italian macaroni manufacturer. When I asked the actor why he had chosen that novel, he told me that the manufacturer's wife had read it and had insisted that it be given on the radio.

Late in 1937 or early in 1938 I was asked to go to Boston, Massachusetts, to take the place of a radio announcer who was ill. Here, two men had a 15 minute daily program on one of the Boston radio stations, in which they gave news bulletins, some music and many commercials praising Italian foods and other products. I could not get used to that type of work and I quit after a day or two.

A few months later (I think it was in March 1938) I was called to Boston once more — this time to work as the editor for the weekly paper *Gazzetta del Massachusetts.* I remained in Boston eight months and on my return to New York found a small job at WOV as a translator of Italian commercials for the Federal Communications Commission.

It was then that I fully realized what most of the Italian programs were. Only a few were interesting and well done. There were some good radio announcers who not only talked well, but used the language correctly. There were some announcers, however, whose only qualification was a pleasant voice. They had no culture and mistreated the language. Because this was noticed by many cultured Italians who strove to preserve the dignity of the language of Dante, I published an article on this subject in *Il*

Carroccio. Later, I wrote a satire in verse castigating the culprits.

Augusto Mauro, a colleague working with me at the *Corriere d'America,* also worked for the radio in his spare time and later full time. When we discussed WOV and other radio stations, he told me that it was useless to write well. "It is better", he said once, "to make as many errors as possible. It seems that that is what the public wants".

Of course, it was not really a question of the public wanting an ungrammatical language. Largely, they just did not realize it was bad. The few who did notice the many errors did not listen to those broadcasts daily. Some plays or sketches were done in Neapolitan or Sicilian dialect. Then, the errors were intentional to be in keeping with the characters.

What appeared objectionable to many listeners were the exaggerations in praising the products that were advertised. This, however, was the common practice and even now we see on TV many unpalatable commercials.

One of these dramatic companies had expropriated a well-known Italian play and, having been threatened with a court action by the author (who resided in Italy and probably acted through an agent) was forced to pay him a considerable sum of money.

It often amazed me that when a short story was read on the radio the author of the story was never mentioned. Usually, only old short stories whose copyright had expired were used, but often stories of contemporary authors would be read. Nobody usually said anything, and nobody bothered to try to identify the authors. One of these stories was adapted by Mauro and myself, by cutting it and reducing it to the required reading time and abolishing all the dialogues. Mauro and I were careful to use old short stories but others took whatever came handy. In Boston I laughed every time Ubaldo Guidi, a well-known speaker, announced: *"Ed ora ecco la promessavi novella",* instead of *"La novella che vi ho promessa".*

Both in Boston and in New York I noticed that speaking over the radio was considered a great accomplishment by many announcers and they had their photographs, with their mouth near the microphone, published in the Italian papers. A New York announcer called himself *"Il principe degli annunziatori".* Actually he was one of the worst offenders, although he did have a nice voice.

Some of the excellent speakers were Stefano and Andrea Luotto, Pietro Novasio (a former Italian deputy), Biagio Farese and many good actors.

Once, a famous actress, Mimi Aguglia, spoke on the radio, but nobody told her that she showed bad taste in allowing herself to be introduced as *"la divina Mimi Aguglia"*.

I had met her once or twice and I had seen her perform wonderfully in several plays. Then she disappeared and once I recognized her in a movie where she had a small part not at all worthy of her past.

When TV came, the Italian radio programs disappeared almost entirely. I had stopped listening many years earlier when, during a strike at WOV I mentioned to the man in charge of the programs that he would do well to have someone check the scripts for errors. Later I learned that the owner of the station had replied that no checking was necessary.

Once Giuseppe Prezzolini appeared on TV for a while, interviewing various prominent people. In an article published in the magazine *Il Borghese* of Milan, Prezzolini had made fun of a local poetaster who had replied with a poem which Prezzolini also published, to the great enjoyment of his readers. Both pieces can be found in his book *I Trapiantati.* That poetaster, whom I mentioned in an article for *Italamerican,* wrote to me asking: "Isn't this the same man who sold macaroni on TV?" I explained to him that Prezzolini did not sell anything: he spoke on a program sponsored by a macaroni manufacturer and that the products were advertised by an announcer.

Immersed in my literary work and the need to earn a living, little time was left for me to worry about my mother, sisters and brother in Italy. And so, the years passed quickly by.

Sometimes, during particularly difficult periods when I was lonesome, pressed by the search for work, tired of some jobs I hated and made unhappy by the privation of family comforts and love, I would be seized by a gripping and painful nostalgia. For many years my earnings were rather meager, especially in the winter months, and most of my savings I sent to my mother. In my spare time I studied hard in the hope of escaping manual labor into which I was first thrust and I soon began writing for several Italian newspapers. I wrote well and I produced some good poetry, but I did not realize that I was making a great mistake. Instead of dedicating my efforts to writing well in English I became an Italian writer. Only later I realized that the Italian press in the United States did not offer a good livelihood to anyone and could not absorb all those who had followed my calling. No job was secure and long-lasting. For short periods of time I found work as an editor of weekly newspapers in several other cities until I went to work for an Italian daily newspaper in New York. I was thirty years old at that time, had become a naturalized citizen and had no immediate desire to return to Italy except for a brief visit. My mother, however, was unhappy. She ardently wished to see me and could not understand why I was not coming back.

After I got married, at 31 years of age, the prospects of visiting Italy receded even further into the future although I continued to write to my mother that eventually I would manage to take a trip and let her meet my wife. It was a promise that I never fulfilled while she was still alive. Not only did my responsibilities increase when my wife gave birth to a boy, but through the evil doings of an ambitious man who had become manager of the newspaper, I lost my job. The depression was then at its peak and my dream of visiting Italy receded still further. It was through this I realized that the separation from the family was the tragedy of practically all the immigrants. I was part of this "nation of immigrants", as John F. Kennedy was to say years later, and had to share the lot of the millions of foreign born Americans who had been forced to detach themselves from their native land. The separation was painful but it was impossible to bridge the gap. When I sent photographs of myself, my wife and my son to my mother, she would be glad, but would cry to my sisters: "I have to be satisfied to see them on paper. I will never see them in person." Gradually, her disappointment increased and she became depressed.

When World War II engulfed the world in a tragedy without precedent, all our hopes of a reunion were dashed. After the invasion of Sicily I lost all contact with my family. At that time I was working as a script writer for the Office of War Information. The entire staff of the Italian section was composed of Italian refugees and a few Americans of Italian extraction whose loyalty to America was unquestioned. While we were wholeheartedly on the Allies side, we could not help but to suffer for what was happening to our native land. We were always the first to learn of the tragic fate of some of our beautiful cities and of the incredible suffering of the population. We prayed and hoped that the Allies would win the war as soon as possible.

With the end of the war, however, the activities of the Office of War Information were drastically curtailed and I was out of a job. Before going there I had worked for some time for the same Italian newspaper that had kicked me out without cause many years before. I had been called back to this paper when Italy entered the war, but soon after that the paper had ceased publication. Gradually the changed conditions and the stoppage of immigration caused many other Italian publications to cease. When I left the Office of War Information I decided to start a small business of my own, but I was alone and without capital and after a long struggle lasting several years I was forced to give it up.

While I still had my business in 1951, I received a letter from Italy informing me that my mother was ill. She had had a stroke and had become paralyzed on one side of her body. It was then that my brother and my sisters pleaded with me to return for a short visit. "Mother has always wished to see you", they wrote. "Now more than ever she suffers for your prolonged absence. She is 77 years old now and very ill. She will not last long. Won't you give her the supreme joy of embracing you before she dies?"

Yes, I wanted to, desperately. After 30 years, however, it was still difficult for me to make the trip. Finally, at the urging of my wife, I decided to go. I managed to find a man who could attend to my business while I was away and I booked passage, writing to my sisters that I would sail at the beginning of February, 1952.

I learned later that my mother clung to the expectation of seeing me and that this prolonged her life for a month or so. The fear that I would reach her bedside too late kept me on edge from the moment I booked passage to the moment I reached my home. The voyage was tediously long and I was uncomfortable with seasickness for some time. When the steamer reached Naples pandemonium broke out aboard because the dock workers were on strike. It was difficult bringing my two suitcases and a package on deck, but I managed and was relieved to see a friend waiting for my landing. He took me to a restaurant and then to his home. That evening I boarded a train and traveled all night. At the Catania railroad station I was greeted by my brother and several cousins one of whom I had left as a boy of seven or eight. Emotion upon emotion shook me. After 31 years neither I nor they were the same persons and I felt a stranger among strangers. Soon my brother and I entered my cousin's little car and he drove up the long, winding road to my hometown, high up in the mountains.

After a while I began to recognize the country I had seen as a boy: the hills all around, the road, the little springs I used to stop by during excursions, the boulders and rocks overhanging the road, some old trees which served as landmarks for the paths I used to take. The past rushed at me from a forgotten time and yet everything seemed strange, uninviting, and almost hostile. Perhaps this was only because I was not in a happy frame of mind, or perhaps it only seemed so because it was winter and nature was dormant. There were a few inches of snow in the town and in the surrounding hills. It was quite cold. I had forgotten that the winter in my hometown was harsh and cruel, with frequent rains, snowstorms, bitter winds and an air of desolation all over. Yet, I had left New York with my usual light undergarments and a rather light suit because our homes are overheated.

A reunion after 31 years of separation is not a happy one. The ravages of time in the persons you had left young and the changes that have occurred in your own body erect a barrier between you and the others. You have become strangers, you are different persons and have little in common. Deep in your heart your ancient love tells you that you must see them as they were when you left them and that you must have the same feelings. Yet, you are uncomfortable and gripped by many mixed emotions.

My mother was lying in bed: a silent and immobile figure with a vacant stare in her eyes. Her face was thin and drawn, with an almost transparent white skin. Her thin, sparse hair was white as snow. I spoke to her but she gave no sign of recognition and for a few minutes I suffered as much as I could stand. I turned from her bed and wept.

"I have come too late", I said to my brother and sisters when I was able to speak. "I should have thought of it and you shouldn't have urged me to come."

One of my sisters said, "She has been like this only since this morning. The certainty of your coming has kept her alive, but it has been a long wait. Yesterday she was able to say a few words and she recognized us. Oh, she has waited so long for this moment!"

It wasn't a reproach. She only wanted to let me know how much my mother had desired to see me. Now there was nothing we could do but wait for the end.

The doctor came a little later and gave her an injection to reanimate her heart, but I knew from his countenance this was in vain.

Desolately I moved in the house, visiting the upper floor and inspecting all the rooms. I went out on the terrace and looked at the hills, the roofs, the houses, the streets. Nothing had changed and yet the streets seemed narrower, the houses smaller, my terrace shrunken. It was a strange feeling. I could not explain this discrepancy between the images I had stored in my memory and the reality. The cold even seemed much more intense than what I remembered. I had not forgotten, but I had become used to our heating system and to the fact that when you walk anywhere in New York you can find relief from the cold in any building, store, or coffee shop. In my hometown the cold was sovereign and I found no relief in any house. The only heat came from a brazier in one room.

The following day around noon my mother came out of her stupor and gave signs of life. Eagerly, tenderly, I spoke to her and she answered my questions with little nods of her head. She still did not pronounce a single word.

"I am sorry I couldn't come sooner", I said. "For years I have wanted to come to see you, but I just couldn't. You must believe me, Mother."

I bent over her head. Suddenly she raised her arm, the one that was not paralyzed, and put it around my neck. I knew then that she had recognized me and had understood and forgiven my long absence. A faint smile hovered over her lips. I stood face to face with her for a few minutes. Then she slowly withdrew her arm, became still again, staring at the ceiling. I did not want her to see the tears that were beginning to fall from my eyes, and I turned away.

From that moment on she gave no sign of consciousness. I knew that the end was near. I had traveled so long and such a distance only for a few minutes of silent communication with her. During the night her breathing became difficult and soon it stopped. I put my ear to her chest and heard the last heartbeats. As soon as the heart became silent I lowered her eyelids and crossed her arms over her chest.

When daylight came we had a visitor, a woman neighbor who soon left and gave the news to other neighbors. Later, everyone remarked that my mother had waited for my return and that she had relented her grip on life as soon as her long-nurtured desire had been satisfied.

Sometime later, back in New York, I tried to express my feelings in a poem which is part of a book I published about twelve years ago.

Last Encounter

You would write, Mother, "The sea
is keeping us apart",
You were too innocent to know
that the whole world is but a raging sea
where the harmless innocent fish
are only prey to monsters.

No friendly ship had I, nor wings except
those of my thoughts clipped
by life inimical.

I know your grief,
humble and bitter, and I disappointed your eagerness
through no fault of mine, for thirty long years.

Your last call
I anxiously heard and hurried
to your side, finally.
You were now a frail branch with scant
and weak lymph. A faint waning light shone
sadly in your eyes.
You saw not the long-awaited son
— now almost an old man — with his heart bent
to your heart.

I stood near you for hours,
and spoke in vain
and hid within me a lifetime of tears.

Then on your wan lips a smile
fluttered: I knew you heard me,
and answered with slight motions
of your tired head,
I thought then that for a few brief moments
a joy supreme
had flooded your heart in the hour extreme.

But soon you became absent,
releasing your hold
on fugitive life — having at last placated
your burning wish.
Your tired lids I lowered
on your spent eyes, and stood
— a bent statue of stone
before your mortal remains —

For your consuming thirst,
O Mother, a single drop.

Giovanni Pinna

The first group of Sardinians to Port Washington where I now live came between the years 1928 and 1930. They were an off-shoot of a larger Sardinian group working in the coal mines of Western Pennsylvania and, like the others, had come to Pennsylvania from the Panama Canal, to which they had emigrated in search of work between 1905 and 1910.

Panama was a favorite target for Sardinian immigrants in the first decade of this century, and both my grandfathers were among those who went there in 1905. The trip was the furthest thing from a pleasure cruise and it was not easy for my grandfathers and the other men to leave their young families behind. The trip had but one purpose for them, to work at what they had been told were good wages, save every possible penny of their earnings, and return home as soon as possible. They knew the risks entailed: the dangers of crossing the Atlantic; and the hazards of Panama's malaria-infested swamps.

The Sardinians had one advantage over other Europeans who helped build the Panama Canal. Sardinia was then, and had been for centuries, infested with malaria, so that its people had built up a certain immunity to the disease. In fact, Mussolini had been so touchy about the existence of malaria in Sardinia that he issued an edict to the effect that malaria was never to be referred to as malaria but must be called "the intermittant fever".

Sardinians are, by nature, reserved and cautious to the point of being suspicious. They tend to feel comfortable only with family and friends.

They are also a people deeply attached to their land. Only a very small percentage of Sardinians venture from the island even for a visit to the mainland Italy. Sardinia, however, is also a poor land and it is difficult to make a living from its rugged soil. Consequently, few Sardinians live a life of ease. They are accustomed to hardships and there are few modern conveniences on the island even now. In my grandfathers' time, living was very primitive so that the privations they encountered in Panama and America did not discourage them. From what they heard, they expected America to be a combination of Eldorado and a vast wilderness. Certainly they hoped to make their fortunes. There was not to be another Gold Rush for them, but they did manage to accomplish what they had set out to do.

As a boy, I showed little interest in the emigration of Sardinians to the Panama Canal, but I recall vividly the reminiscences of Nonno Luigi, who was my mother's father and my favorite grandparent.

Today, the town of Pattada from which my grandfathers left for America seventy years ago and from which I myself, came in 1963, is only two hours by car from the nearest seaport called Olbia. In my grandfathers' time it took not less than a day to get there by donkey. Olbia was known then as Terranoa, and "Terranoa" is to this day the Sardinian name for America. Nonno Luigi liked to say that he and his brother, Demetrio (for my grandfathers were brothers), had set out from America to go to America. It was quite a favorite family joke.

Although Terranoa was then, and is now, one of the thriving seaports of Italy, passage to the mainland was most unreliable and one might have to wait days for a liner. It was much easier to bypass the mainland by hitching a boat ride across the Strait of Bonifacio to the island of Corsica.

Nonno Luigi often told of how they boarded a vessel at Terranoa, stopped at Ajaccio, the capital city of Corsica, and again at Marseilles. His recollection of the harbor at Marseilles was vivid, but he was even more excited by the memory of Barcelona where he and his *compari* disembarked from one boat to board a larger vessel for the transatlantic trip. On the pier at Barcelona, he was much impressed by a monument of Christopher Columbus that had been erected at one end of the pier. Columbus stood tall upon a soaring column and pointed his outstretched arm to the West. "I could only see his back", Nonno Luigi told me excitedly, "for you see, I was going westward myself"!

My grandfather was less enthusiastic about the ocean voyage. He remembered feeling uneasy about the vastness of the sea that seemed as though it would never end. He liked to joke about how different it might have been had all those gallons of seawater been wine mellowed in his own vats to be measured out in comradeship to his fellow travellers. After a week of rough weather on the high seas, Pattada's vineyards seemed lost in time and the initial euphoria of the group dampened. The adventurers felt suspended between their homes and their hopes for the future. "How I missed my wife and child," Nonno said, "But, thanks to God and Our Lady of the Carmines, we arrived".

The Pinna brothers left Sardinia in the month of March, 1905, and returned the following winter. There were, in all, forty-one *paesani* from Pattada on board the ship and the group included my paternal grandmother's brother as well. My grandfathers felt more encouraged entering a strange situation with such a sizeable group of closely-knit relatives and neighbors. The north wind (called the *Travuntana* by Sardinians and known as the *Tramontana* in Italian) was sweeping away the cold of winter and the air was crisp in Pattada when the group left for Panama. It was April and the air was strangely heavy with tropical heat and humidity when they arrived in the Canal Zone. Rain beat with an alien rhythm on the canvas tents provided by the company as living quarters for the construction gangs. Accustomed to rough living, my grandfathers adjusted to the hardships and Luigi's superior skills as a builder were soon recognized and his wages increased. The brothers worked on the Canal construction for nine months, but by then they were growing restless. They had worked off their obligation to the company for their passage and had put aside enough savings to justify their trip. Many years later I learned what happened next when my parents were considering moving our family to America. Out of respect for his age and position in our family, they asked my grandfather's opinion on emigration.

Typically, my grandfather prefaced his reply with an anecdote which nicely illustrates the Sardinian quirks of public relations.

On his departure from Pattada, Nonno Luigi had been given a pair of boots by Zizzu Mannu Chessa (the shoemaker of Pattada) which he had made for his son, John. John Chessa, who lives today in Armonk, New York, had left Pattada in 1903 for Panama. My grandfather searched for him when he, himself, arrived there in 1905. However, the earlier group of Sardinians had already left Panama for North America in search of a permanent life with better wages and living quarters more sympathetic to Sardinian ways. They sent word to their *compari* remaining in Panama that work was available in the coal mines of western Pennsylvania. In the company of other Sardinians, Luigi and Demetrio headed north to

Philadelphia and eventually reached the mining town of Shenandoah where they found John Chessa. Nonno Luigi delivered the boots entrusted to his care by Zizzu Mannu Chessa and, years later he would wink and say that he had kept his word and fulfilled his obligation to deliver those boots even though it had taken him around the world!

The story of the boots told, Nonno Luigi then explained that he had found the tents of Panama so vulnerable to the weather and so different from the almost cave-like security of Sardinian houses built of stone and mortar that he was delighted to leave them. The one-story wooden dwellings provided by the mining company in Pennsylvania were an improvement over the tents even though they were without heat or running water. Running water in the homes of Pattada did not materialize until 1953, so this particular hardship did not alarm my grandfathers. As a matter of fact, the wooden structure used as a communal latrine was more than they were used to at home. Even in my own youth in Pattada we all, regardless of age, would go to the rocks at the end of town to *pro su bisonzu.*

An indoor privy, however, did not make up for the absence of a house made of stone and warmed by a massive fireplace that so dominates the Sardinian home that it is almost a member of the family. To make things more intolerable, Nonno Luigi was a master stonecutter and wooden houses left him philosophically as well as physically cold. Moreover, the promised high wages proved to be lower than those paid by the construction company in Panama, so that after a brief consideration of bringing their families to America for permanent immigration, Luigi and Demetrio seized upon the first opportunity for passage home. Curiously, neither of my grandfathers considered the possibility of building a home of his own in the company town.

Some of their group returned with them to Sardinia while others stayed behind. Other Sardinians arrived in Pennsylvania after my grandfathers had left, and the year 1912 saw the largest number of Sardinian immigrants arrive to work in Panama. According to Mimmia Frommigia, whose interview follows, by 1915 the peak number of 200 Sardinian families lived in the United States. There are fewer here today, for the usual cycle of the Sardinian immigrant repeats the experience of my grandfathers: to work hard, save every possible penny, and return to the homeland. Others have chosen to return for their families or to acquire a Sardinian wife, and come back to America with their own families or with the relatives of fellow immigrants living in the United States. The Sardinian immigrant rarely returns alone and his ties with his place of birth are upheld with an almost religious fervor.

The life experience of one such Sardinian immigrant, Mimmia Frommigia, spans the whole period of emigration from our island. He too lives in Port Washington, although, like all Sardinians, he is reluctant to talk about himself.

Mimmia Frommigia has lived in the United States for more than 50 years, almost all of which were spent in Port Washington. It was not easy to interview Mimmia, for he is 83 years old and in poor health. He frequently shook his head and said, "I've lost my mind" (meaning his memory) and frankly admitted that he often did not recognize people when his wife had to remind him of my identity.

Nevertheless, after our first glass of wine, "Tiu Mimmia" began to apologize: "This wine is not so tasty", he said, "because I did not make it myself this year. This is the first year that I have not made wine. I did not feel up to it". The following interview was basically a conversation beginning with my assurances that the wine, though certainly not so fine as the one he had made himself, was good and most welcome. We spoke at all times in Sardinian, which is a separate language from Italian and is much more consonated. With the traditional respect due him because of his advanced age, I addressed Mimmia as "Tiu Mimmia". This translates into Italian as "Zio Giova Maria" and into English as "Uncle John". I think much is lost in the translation. For me to call him "Tiu" or "Uncle" although he is not related to me by blood is only another example of the closeness and formality of the Sardinian people. The "G" of the interview which follows, stands for "Giovanni" which I sadly relinquished years ago for the Americanization, John. To "Tiu Mimmia" I will always be Giovanni, and I suspect that I am, myself, doomed to a lifetime of looking for someone else when "John" is called.

A resident of the United States for 53 years, Tiu Mimmia first emigrated to the United States in 1914. In 1915 he returned to Italy as a recruit in the Italian army and did not re-emigrate to the United States until 1919.

Tiu Mimmia obviously enjoyed telling me about his achievements as a soldier. The slow tempo of his speech quickened as he told of his arrival in Genoa. Having presented himself at the nearest induction center, he was given the proper uniform, the rank of sergeant, and a three-day pass, which he used to go home to Pattada by over-night boat. He had been assigned to an artillery outfit as a platoon sergeant.

G.   How is it you were made sergeant on your first day in the army? I was in Vietnam for a whole year and all I got to be was a corporal!

M: Ah, Giovanni, you must take heart! Remember that Napoleon was only a "little corporal" at the beginning. But for me; that was not my first day in the army. I had fought in Turkey for one year and I was stationed in Libya for two and a half years before coming to the United States in 1914.

At this point, "Tiu Mimmia" poured us each, another glass of wine and continued the account of his heroics in the "First War". His unit had included a large group of Sardinians with whom he enjoyed a special *comaraderie*. But, he remarked, the best times were when his troop joined in the fighting with the "Sa Brigade Tattaei", one of the most glorious infantry units in the Italian army. The "Sa Brigade Tattaei" was based in Sardinia and, as Mimmia put it; "That infantry brigade was made up of Sardinian soldiers from its general, 'su Generale Cossu' to the last private in the ranks!"

Could more be said? By now, Mimmia was on his feet, pointing to the medals and citations hanging on the wall of his den. He had been cited, one plaque read, for "single-handedly blowing-up two German cannons. More than half a century later, in 1971, the Italian government gave Mimmia the title of *"Cavaliere all'Ordine di Vittorio Veneto"* (Knight Cavalier of the Order of Victor Veneto) for his conspicuous bravery in blowing up the cannons. He was awarded a pension of *"40 iscudos onzi ses meses"*, which amounts to $40.00 every six months. So much for war profits.

Luckily, Mimmia does not have to live on his Italian pension. His house is comfortable, even spacious, and on a treelined street which, as might be expected, has three other Sardinian families. He lives alone, there, with his second wife, Giuanna Maria. With typical Sardinian concern for family things and with a directness that can be uncomfortable if you are the object, she never fails to upbraid me for being single. As reticent as Sardinians can be among strangers, there is nothing to compare with the clarity of their inquisition among friends.

Giuanna Maria and Mimmia were both widows when they married in 1953, Giuanna Maria and her first husband had also emigrated from Pattada.

Giuanna Maria explained that, as is the custom, her husband-to-be was in the United States for a few years before she came here to marry him. It was arranged that she stay in the home of Pedru Dettori, a fellow immigrant from Pattada, properly chaperoned by his family during the few weeks that preceeded their marriage. Of Mimmia's first wife she only said: "Mimmia had been married also...to an Italian, but she was not from Sardinia. She died in childbirth".

For Mimmia Frommigia and Giuanna Maria to marry was the most sensible and natural thing to do and it was, of course, in the finest Sardinian tradition. When still another glass of wine had been poured, this time for Giuanna Maria as well, I was tempted to ask "Tiu Mimmia" whether he had continued to make his own wine during Prohibition, but I decided that he would be offended by any suggestion that a Sardinian would break the law. For the same reason I avoided asking his opinion concerning the notorious bandits of Sardinia, although it was rumored that one of his Port Washington neighbors had been one. Benito Mussolini was so determined to camouflage all blemishes upon the face of his regime that, along with the rigid avoidance of malaria as a subject, he ordered the press that there was to be no reference made to the always present Sardinian bandits.

When Mimmia left for the war in 1915, he had been accompanied by two other emigrants. Afterwards, one was killed in combat and the other decided to remain in Sardinia. In 1919 he returned alone to the mine fields of Shenandoah, Pennsylvania, where my grandfather had delivered the boots to John Chessa. There was another colony of Sardinians in the nearby town of Minersville, and Mimmia claims to have been a prime mover in the decision of a group drawn from both mining towns, to come to Long Island. They came to the "Sand Bank", in Port Washington which was doing a thriving business stripping layers of sand from the steep hills overlooking Roslyn Harbor. An entire railroad system threaded its way through the embankment then, and manual labor was the core of the production. Today, the railroad system is gone and production is greatly reduced. Manual labor has been replaced by machines and only a handful of workers remain. The Sardinians among the present workers still refer to the company as the *So Banchina* as did the earliest arrivals.

Mimmia avoided answering questions concerning his personal welfare and whether he had been discriminated against by members of other ethnic groups. He would not discuss his earnings, but mentioned that in the midst of the Depression, he was paid 10 cents an hour to chop wood in Worchester, Massachusetts, and that his pay had climbed drastically to 25 cents an hour when he crossed into Vermont.

It was with obvious pride that Mimmia Frommigia told me about his role in the Icanusa Society. He had founded the organization in 1942, when he interested 45 other Sardinians in forming a group. As the founder he was elected the Society's first president and served in that capacity for two years. With the Council, or *Consiglieri,* he proposed dues of one dollar a month, which were used to help with the funeral expenses of a deceased member and to give $200.00 to the bereaved family.

He also persuaded his boss at *So Banchina* to let the group use a large "shanty" there, with whatever furniture ·it contained, for Labor Day weekends. He recounted:

> Sardinians would come from Connecticut, Detroit and Pennsylvania...even on trucks...for a three day feast! That was when we were more unified than we are now. If one received news *dae Idda* (meaning from Pattada) we used to pass the news to all the others. We used to see each other more often; we helped each other and supported each other any way we could. Sometimes it would be just moral support, but if one of us was in need, we used to take up a collection. If there was a new arrival, we all tried to make him welcome, and it was the custom, when one of us was going to Sardinia, to send a gift of money through him to his relatives and to give him a *bon voyage* gift as well.

G: Tiu Mimmia, I have heard so many good things about the "Ichanusa Society" that I am honored to hear about its early days from the founder, himself. Tell me, does it still exist?

M: No. By 1964 we were left with only seven paying members, Pedru DeJana was president, then, and we voted to dissolve the Society.

Mimmia Frommigia, at 83, represents the first wave of Sardinian immigrants to the United States. He thinks and lives as a Sardinian. He has never attempted to become "Americanized" although he is fiercely loyal to his adopted country. I would not have dared, however, to ask him if he is an American citizen, for such a question would have been disrespectful considering the difference in our ages and my comparative recent immigration.

Tiu Mimmia does, however, represent an attitude of isolation from the mainstream of American life which is in sharp contrast to the aggressive way in which the Society's last president is going about the business of assimilation.

Pedru DeJana, too, is a Sardinian immigrant and, like Mimmia and myself, a native of Pattada. When he arrived in the United States with his father, Nanneddu, in 1954, they were welcomed by many *paesani*...by

Nanneddu's brother, Andria, and his brother-in-law, Pedru Dettori, and by many other relatives. Pedru, then 15 years old, took the advice of his uncles and enrolled in Port Washington High School, where his cousins were already studying. He had taken the first step towards becoming an American.

Nanneddu worked in *So Banchina* five days a week and, on Saturdays, he worked for a gardener with his son Pedru, who by now was called either "Peter" or "Pete". Their boss was also from Sardinia, although not from our home town. He returned to Sardinia in 1959, but his memory lingers on in a favorite story told by his *compari* in Port Washington. They swear that at one of their gatherings, he volunteered to take on a job of cooking an entire side of beef which had been purchased jointly for the occasion. The cooking went on all day, as did the drinking of aperitifs. Every so often someone would ask him if the meat were ready and he would reply, pointing to a still rare part of the gigantic roast, "Not yet, no, not yet. Have another drink". When the wine had disappeared and the mellowed group turned hungrily to their roasted beef, the self-appointed "cook" had eaten it all.

Peter DeJana's younger brother, Phil, was called Tillippu when he was my classmate in Pattada. Now, like his brother but unlike me, he speaks English without a trace of an accent, having come to America at the age of nine. Like Pete, he too is a graduate of Port Washington High School. Only Vincent, their younger brother, has been to college, and he left after one year. Both brothers work in Pete's growing business.

When Tillippu, his mother, his two sisters and Vincent arrived in America three years after Nanneddu and Pete, the transplanting of the DeJana family to Port Washington was complete. Far from being "uprooted", to use Oscar Handlin's famous description of immigration to the United States, the DeJana stock is flourishing.

In the American tradition, Pete DeJana has made his money work to make more money, living without ostentation and expanding his business at every opportunity. He now holds contracts for the maintenance of roads in four villages. His only apparent luxury is his passion for expensive automobiles. From a purple Corvette he has graduated to a red sports Mercedes, not to mention a Cadillac and a bright yellow Jeepster. His modest living quarters are in the best tradition of Sardinian immigrants, who, like his own family, lived in the simple, frame houses of the Sand Bank complex. If Mimmia Frommigia's comfortable home is any indication of the rewards for hard work, Pedru DeJana will wind up in a mansion.

When I came to the United States as an immigrant in 1963, I was sponsored by my father's sister, who, like Mimmia Frommigia, thought more in Sardinian terms than in American despite her long years of residence here. Unlike Pete DeJana's uncles who had encouraged him to enter high school, my aunt urged me to get right to work and bring in money. Without specific training and having almost no command of English, the jobs I could get were all unskilled. I worked as a gardener, as a gas station attendant, and, with a little guidance from my boss, as a mechanic. My wages were at the minimum levels, but, since I worked overtime and often at several jobs at a time, I was quite content with the situation from a financial viewpoint. There is a large Italian population in Port Washington (in addition to the Sardinian group) so that by socializing almost exclusively with them, I felt quite comfortable about my lack of English. Except for words and phrases learned in the street or picked up by deciphering captions under photographs in the papers, I made no effort to learn the language. Just as Nonno Luigi had joked that he and his brother had "Left America to come to America". I had, for all practical purposes, left Italy to come to Italy. Looking back, I know that only my body was here in America; my thoughts, concerns for the future, and my deepest feelings were all in Sardinia.

All that was changed when I was drafted into the United States Army in 1968. By then I was 23 years old and had still not decided whether I intended to stay in America. I was not a citizen, and somehow I felt that the Vietnam war had nothing to do with me. Yet, there I was, after basic training, right up at the front line, serving in the 173 Airborne Brigade. I think it was the strong feelings of comradeship which I felt with my buddies that made me decide I wanted to stay in America if I ever came out of Vietnam alive. They were the first Americans I had gotten to know well, other than Italian Americans, and it felt good to be accepted even with my strong accent. For that matter, the differences between southern accents and those from the Midwest or the East were so great, that I felt more comfortable about my own. Now that I had made my decision to be an American and was in the thick of a shooting war, I was determined to get my citizenship. It took a bit of doing to cut the red tape involved, but in March, 1970, I became a citizen of the United States.

~FOUR~
The
Theater People

Introduction

By the late nineteenth and early twentieth centuries immigrant theater had come to be closely associated with the cultural baggage of "new immigrant" peoples. As a medium of expression, the Italian theater reflected the new society through the familiar dramatic themes of the old country. This apparently comported with the interests of the audiences which sought romantic, emotional and spirited performances rather than philosophical debates, intellectual challenges or social criticism. The themes of the Italian theater emphasized simplicity, purity and the dramatic as performances elicited responses from the pathos of human drama.

With the foreign press and national schools, each immigrant group which entered the United States sought to perpetuate its heritage also through the theater. Thus, although the Italian theater never achieved the influences of the Yiddish theater, for example, it did play an important role in the cultural lives of the Italians in their American surroundings.

Theatrical performances at the turn of the century were staged in churches, or in social clubs and coffee houses some of which later became theater clubs where performances were held on Sundays and holidays. Many of the actors and actresses volunteered their performances as a labor of love, having non-theatrical full-time jobs from which they derived their livelihoods. Eventually, some theatrical companies formed and developed the expertise to bring the immigrant theater from the Eastern seaboard to the "Little Italies" throughout the nation.

Clara Grillo was the daughter of an Italian boarding-house owner and the wife of a theatrical impressario. Her autobiography details the career of her husband who rented and managed several Italian theaters in Cleveland,

Ohio. Through the course of the career of her husband, Clara Grillo came to know the Italians in the Little Italy of Cleveland and many other Little Italies throughout the country, thereby observing the life of the larger Italian community when it came to this aspect of the ethnic group's culture.

The story of Clara Grillo relates the atmosphere of an Italian American theater family as it also describes the story of her own career as an educator. Between the stories of her father and husband, Clara Grillo comments from the vantage point of the old world as well as the American culture.

Urbane, articulate and educated, Julian Miranda, the second account of this chapter, is as familiar with American society as he is with his Sicilian roots. His love of both the land of his ancestors and his own country although manifest is not blind to the foibles of both Italian and American societies. His background is so varied that he could have been included in several of the chapters of this text. I chose to include him among the theater accounts because he is one of the few articulate men who were participants in this movement. As such, he provides a clear insight into the role of the Italian theater and Italian radio with an honesty which permits us to see the vices as well as the virtues.

Clara Corica Grillo

My father, Francesco Corica, was born July 29, 1873, in Sinagra, Messina, in feudal-steeped Sicily during a difficult economic period. When his father, Antonio Corica died while my father was still a youth, my father's godfather "Il Barone Sa Leo" the local baron directed my father to take on the support of the family which included his mother, Rosa Rosaria (nee Pullella) and seven brothers and sisters. Consequently, my father's education was very limited and he never learned to read or write although he had tried to attend night classes. Sinagra, however, is located in the hills of Messina and the river which had to be crossed to get to the distant school was often impassable. One spring my father fell into the river which was then swollen with melting snows and heavy currents. Badly frightened, he never returned to school.

When he decided to come to America, my father chose to settle in Cleveland, Ohio since it had been the destination of earlier Sinagrese migrants, including our cousin Leo Coppolino who had an *agenzia commerciale* (a bilingual agency serving newly arrived immigrants). The only knowledge my father had of the new country was that a man who was not afraid to work could do well — a condition which was not true of Sicily's *terra brucciata* (scorched earth).

I do not know all the details or arrangements for the ship voyage, but I do remember my father saying he had little money left after lending money to his cousin Francesco Piraino, for his expenses and paying for himself, my mother (nee Carmela Bonfiglio) and my sister Rosa (18 months old).

After traveling from his home to Palermo, my father boarded a boat to Naples. Finally, after much fear and misery, the sick, and vomiting passengers were transported from Naples to New York. Eventually, they arrived in Cleveland, Ohio, scared, ill, and disoriented.

No problems other than language and rough handling were encountered by my father at the hands of merchants or government officials. He was happy to have reached his goal where, contrary to "golden" expectations, the streets were not even paved. At this point he intended only to work, make money, and hurry back to his family. My mother had also wished to return since she missed her brother, Carmelo Bonfiglio, who was her closest relative since her mother and father had died before she married. My mother had come from a proud family that impressed upon her that no one who sought her hand was good enough for her. After all, she was healthy, a virgin, a fine seamstress, especially of hand-stitched wedding gowns, an expert and quick olive picker and well-liked for her beautiful singing voice, which made her popular in the tedious tasks of the olive groves. Her friends said her voice took their fatigue away so they encouraged her to sing and dumped their olives into her homemade willow cannisters to help her earn her quota for the day.

The homemade furniture was left in the patriarchal homestead high up in the mountains of Messina. It was a valuable piece of land because it had a natural well of water and good, cultivated soil. My father had intended to leave the property for family use for the duration of his mother's life and then divide it among his seven brothers and sisters with, of course, a portion for himself. One relative, a cousin, Rosario Pullella (who wore a gold earring to insure good eyesight) was quite upset when my father would not sell the land to him. Following my uncle's demise which, although never authenticated, most likely occurred when he was reputed missing after capture in Austria-Hungary during World War I, his wife, my Aunt Maria, married her nephew, Antonio Musca, another cousin of ours. I recall sending an enlarged tinted photo of Uncle Vincenzo to Sinagra to be hung in the local schoolhouse, *nell'aula*. Later, Aunt Marie and Antonio "Nino" Musca moved to Australia where they stayed several years only to return to Sinagra where it was they who finally bought my father's share of the family estate.

I saw those members of my family when I traveled to Italy for the first time in 1933. My cousins were dressed in the fascist style, used the fascist salute, and sang the currently popular songs of the era. The eldest son of Maria Corica and Vincenzo Corica was named Antonio Corica after our mutual paternal grandfather. Antonio was also reported missing in action somewhere in Russia during World War II. He had been an elementary school teacher as were his four brothers and sisters. Later, one of them became a lawyer, and then a county judge.

When my father emigrated, he and his family were required to travel down the mountain on foot and/or donkey back. From this mountainous ˉegion, it was then necessary to get to the sea. I clearly recall how excited ˌe town was, in 1933, when the only fish that reached Sinagra had been ˌserved for me during my visit at Uncle Carmelo's home. Carmelo was ˅ father's oldest brother and, after a stay in the United States, he ˌurned to Italy intending to convert the Catholics to Pentacostalism. ˀd, however, he married a thirty year old woman and wasted away in with little impact on the community's deepseated Catholicism. ˈˉncle Carmelo took on the old ways. His wife had even pushed ˌipod he had arranged to enable her to stand as she cooked. She ˌstead, to stir the food, and cook it over a low fire, dragging ˈ s skirts on the dirty ashes.

ˌrred that Uncle Carmelo should fix things up for his wife, ˌˌ abandoned tripod and said he had tried, but that she did not wish to change. I smiled when I noted that while she was stubborn, he too refused to change his ways. They still slept on large planks over which they tossed a flattened homespun linen mattress stuffed with corn husks. The bag-like cover had elongated slits permitting the entry of a hand to stir the contents. Everything was rough linen, the flax of which had been grown at home, the thread spun and woven at home, and the material dyed as in the days of my mother who had often described this to me. Indeed, my mother had even followed much the same pattern at the beginning of her stay in America.

The attitudes of the Italians who remained in Italy when my father departed was "Blessed *(beato)* are you who can leave this hopeless land. May God bless you." Further, they begged my mother and father to send letters telling what it was really like in America. How much did food cost? How much were shoes? Were there many bridges? Was the water good? Did they have silkworms? Did the women have to work in the fields? Was the cold unbearable? Were the *padroni* (bosses) mean? Did they live near a church? When would they come back? "Don't", they begged, "don't forget to provide for your parents. God will always bless you." Many women asked them to look up husbands who had gone on ahead and established new families in America, completely abandoning the ones in Italy.

Breaking lifelong ties with home, family, friends and familiar surroundings was poignant. Tears, fearful thoughts, and absurd, but well meant promises were made and broken by my parents with the single exception of my father's vow to support his mother until her death. He also supported my mother, her brother and contributed to the village church.

The greatest, most overpowering fear of mother during the voyage was that the roughness and rolling of the sea would be her death. She related how the passengers in the crowded steerage class lamented their condition, prayed aloud and called on God night and day to save them from the monsters in the waters. There were also offensive smells and lice. The food on board ship was plentiful, but not well prepared.

The ship landed in New York, where the emigrants went through physical examinations. Many had to be deloused. All of the immigrants were given the opportunity to bathe, but they were unaccustomed to baths and some would only bathe their feet. Some of the women never had washed their hair before or after coming to America. The men went to the showers and rough-housed. No one met my parents, although they received information from cousin Leo Coppolino, who now had a notary public agency and lived at 1991 E. 126th Street, in Cleveland. Other *paesani* also lived nearby there.

My father's impression, upon meeting the earlier immigrant groups, was that they were all in the same situation. They were intelligent but ignorant of American ways so they were at a disadvantage. People could easily take advantage of them especially those of their own kind. Outwardly these people treated my father with respect because he had been taught good manners, and he respected himself.

With the immigrants there was much rivalry among people from the various parts of Italy. Thus, even those born in America, would perpetuate it such as: *Campobassiani, mangia patani, cide pidocchi e suona campane* (People from Campobasso; are potato eaters, lice killers and bell ringers). Those from other provinces substituted "Siciliani" for "Campobassiani". This regional rivalry still prevails to several generations.

The social status of the parents and even grandparents figured in all kinds of business deals and friendships in America. I was much sought after as a godmother since, as a high school teacher, I could intercede with American governmental agencies, the police, schools, etc. I even received at least a dozen marriage proposals because I could be useful to 'guys' and 'racketeers'. I told everybody I was never going to get married. I only wanted to teach.

Immigrant newcomers who came after my father was established had a hard time too, but many of the earlier immigrants had attained enough economic status to help the later ones. The newer wave also came to relatives and better jobs.

The most serious privations and trials of my father's immigrant group were the loneliness, lack of grandparents and in-laws and the disorientation and mutilation of the family group. This led to a feeling of complete estrangement. However, there was so much to do just to earn a living, and keep a job, that maybe his generation felt the absence of relatives less than mine has. Generally, they were all so physically fatigued from daily labors that they simply got drunk, slept, rose and started the day again. Basically, they were happy knowing that every effort brought in money, perhaps not much, but many, many times better than they had been used to.

The women also liked not having to be subordinate to the mother-in-law as they were in Europe. Then, as families became established here, the old tribal bug-a-boos were re-established. The bossy grandparents, in-laws, and critical neighbors reappeared in group relations. So, the Italians, as they prospered, left the Italian community and became more involved in "American" activities.

Some of them became involved in politics in a dubious way. I remember one story, which used to be told about the political campaigns of neighborhood councilmen candidates, who would tear up Kinsman Road and rebuild it at election time. This became a joke to those of us who were aware of politics, but this kind of situation was more likely to take place among the generation of Italian Americans who preceded my father's generation rather than in my childhood. The Democratic Party seemed to be the dominant one in the Little Italies we knew, however, my father was, I believe, not interested at all in this.

Many Italians in Cleveland's Little Italy were impressed with the fact that being a lawyer or judge would help get better treatment in American society, and many were consequently motivated to study law.

The most common problem of family adjustments that caused great trouble was the freedom given to females in the United States. Even coeducation was terrifying to the first immigrants. I personally have case histories of how girls were not allowed to attend English and/or citizenship classes. This problem was especially true among Sicilian families whose conduct was subject to many taboos. Rules of courtship, marrying of people from other parts of Italy or from other nationality groups, from other religions, or from the lower social strata, all were (and still are) problems.

My father's attachment to the old country lasted only while his mother was alive. When she died, he really abandoned things Italian since he spoke enough English to get along. When he was nearing 80 years of age, however, he became lonesome for his Italian friends and family and he even returned to church services. He had no membership in clubs although I still maintain the old ties with "Little Italy" via correspondence and visits.

The first house rented by my parents was about two doors away from the Mayfield Theater. It was the front house, the backyard of which housed the local wine press. Among the important institutions in the neighborhood was the Holy Rosary Church, established in 1860, whose priest called personally for donations.

Not long after we moved there, we discovered the Alta House located on the corner of E. 125th Street and Mayfield Road. This institution is no longer serving that community of "Little Italy" (1974) through health programs, athletics, dramatics, playgrounds, club meetings and classes. Even the Cleveland Public Library received its superb collection of Italian books in the Foreign Literature Section of the Main Branch from Alta House. Being illiterate both my father and mother never went there. Both were obsessed with work. They had utilized only the tonsil clipping clinic. They had no time for socials or recreation or education. The church, Alta Settlement House (said to be named after a daughter of John D. Rockefeller) and Murray Hill School, all offered much help to the newcomers. The Alta House was a settlement house established by the Rockefellers under Protestant direction. As such, the Holy Rosary Catholic Church priests did not approve but a number of Italians went there despite this. Alta tried to Americanize immigrants, stressing health, cleanliness, nutrition, crafts, sports, and American citizenship. Since the old rickety, clapboard houses in Little Italy had only the most basic plumbing, and were without bathtubs or showers, many used the Alta facilities. Our boarders for example, bathed at the Alta House on Saturdays. For ten cents they received a clean towel, soap, and a shower. Often they played *bocce* there.

In Alta House women learned to sew, embroider and care for themselves when pregnant in prenatal clinics after which they later attended the baby clinics there. For school children the settlement house provided tonsil clipping clinics, sports, swings and baseball. Dancing parties and even citizenship preparation classes and English classes met there. All tended to "Americanize" recent arrivals — the vogue of social workers then.

There was also in Cleveland a Citizenship Bureau, the International Institute branch of the Y.W.C.A. and the Cleveland Board of Education which conducted bilingual classes to help immigrants become citizens. Immigrant women were provided with interpreters when applying for charity, specialized clinics for eyecare and rare diseases or for welfare. Americanization was intended to make us forget our Italian roots since anything "foreign" was suspect. Yet, nobody bothered to stop and explain to us what was wrong or right. Consequently, we were seldom welcome in established communities. Social workers played a prominent role in our Americanization although the oldest Italian population was not easily influenced.

The Catholic Church was the most important influence although a Protestant church existed near the Murray Hill school. The latter's progress was unheralded. Everything centered around the Holy Rosary parish.

My father's first impression of his first employment in the New World was favorable since the pay for laying railroad ties and digging ditches was, by Sicilian standards, exceedingly high. The $1 to $1.50 per day wages seemed munificent.

John D. Rockefeller offered him a job but my father's background led him to refuse the offer to work for the same lowly wages as the others. My father knew he worked as much as two or even three men and he reasoned that he would not gain anything by leaving the *paesani* to work for the rich man who had made such a bargain. My father worked for similar overseers in Sicilian estates and wished to get away from them completely. He did not get involved with unions, socialists, anarchists, or similar groups, steering clear of them, priests, and insurance companies because he was suspicious of all their motives.

My father settled on Mayfield Road, in the Little Italy of Cleveland, Ohio, where over 90 percent of the neighborhood was Italian immigrants. We lived at 1929 E. 126th Street until the nearby Lakeview Cemetery was enlarged to such an extent that my mother could look into open graves from our kitchen window. Our house was close to Garfield's Monument.

My parents' home housed twenty-six boarders. These men were engaged mostly as ditch diggers, railroad laborers and steel mill helpers. There were also a few gardeners. After a day's work and a heavy meal, they rough-housed in the back yard in good weather and played accordions, flutes, and leap frog. Since my father ran the house with harsh discipline, they conformed to his rules. Lights were out at 9:00 p.m. and anyone not inside by then was locked out. Occasionally, they wrote duty letters back home which were frequently dictated to me (I was eleven years old then). The message was always the same:

Dear Mother,

I take pen in hand to let you know I am in good health and hope to hear the same from you. My regards and big kisses to _____(then followed the traditional roll call).

Aside from letter writing for which I charged ten cents, I often went to the saloon to buy beer for pennies. I stood near the door and, as I handed the nickel and the tin to the bartender, I peered into the exciting interior. It was hectic, noisy and smelly. The piles of hard cooked eggs, mounds of *ciceri* (chick peas) and *fave* (beans), salted and roasted, were part of my pay. I munched these as I swung the tin pail brimming with foam. I never lost a drop of beer as I hurried home happy. From the few pennies I hoarded $117.00, which became the foundation of my college education.

Most of the men who boarded with my father were *paesani* from my father's village and he was a father figure to them. He even disciplined them. I remember one cousin being slapped by my father after he had lost money playing cards. When boarders intervened my cousin said, "Leave him alone. He has a right to slap me".

These men were hard workers. They left home as daylight came up, and walked to their jobs to save the three cents carfare. One or two rode their bicycles to work. They earned a dollar a day, or at most, a dollar and a half.

For fun they often played cards or *mora,* a guessing game of how many fingers two players totaled as they spread out and showed their fingers. Simultaneously they would yell *"Cinque, Otto"* etc. Sometimes a third party kept score and the winner downed a glass of wine which made the players rather jolly on a long winter evening.

At times they played leap frog in the backyard and became quite boisterous riding each other. Sometimes they fought each other and rough-housed. Several men played homemade, hand carved flutes. Others had brought mandolins, accordions and guitars from Italy.

Drinking freshly-squeezed grape juice, held in fifty gallon whiskey kegs, had the effect of turning our boarders into operatic stars or lovelorn singers. Their favorites were *Ciribiribi, Santa Lucia,* and *La Donn'e Mobile.* Listening to Italian American records that poked fun at "greenhorns" was also widely enjoyed. In this connection the comical character was usually someone named *Nofriu,* a character who was confused or exploited by his *paesani.* Some men just whittled away their time.

Next to eating, drinking and playing cards, the boarders liked to dance. Often the men danced with one another because there were not enough females. The men clomped about in mazurkas, polkas, fast dances and very few waltzes. They talked, laughed, sweated profusely and seemed to enjoy the dances as endurance challenges. They only stopped when the musicians quit or when my father chased them all to bed, saying *"Basta, basta, domani si travaglia. A dormire tutti".*

Next to the Mayfield Theater there was a dry good store owned by a Jew, which was later operated by Michael Mastandrea. Mike's bait was a never ending succession of sales on the grounds that he was going to sell out and return to Italy, which he never did. Instead he entered the theater business after taking over the Mayfield Theater. By the time he died he was a successful showman and salesman, respected by the community in spite of his advertising schemes. His children and others turned the theater into an institution for legitimate stage productions with vaudeville, Italian films, and American films, both silent and talkies. My husband exhibited shows, vaudeville and films there. It was a small and intimate theater and lasted until December 1974. It is now run, however, as a nostalgic rerun film house.

My husband put on many legitimate productions such as *Commedia dell'Arte.* He would book traveling actors who were, for the most part, poor, but proud, professionals. Whenever we were broke my husband would rely on a tear jerker such as *Senza Mama e' Namurato* which would inevitably play to full houses for long runs. Show parlance, however, called it 'crap'.

Outstanding among the actors Caveliere Eduardo Migliaccio, whose stage name was *Farfariello,* was highly educated and spoke and wrote in English, French and Italian including many dialects. His forte was *macchieta* skits which ridiculed immigrant types such as the president of the Sons of Italy. It would take a book merely to list *Farfariello's* contributions to Italo-American culture. For four decades he was on stage all over America. Among his lasting contributions were the movies made by him at Columbia University on the "Language of Gesture" referred to by H.L. Mencken in his text, *American Language.* Professor Prezzolini of Columbia's Casa Italiana has one chapter in his book and a few photographs of *Farfariello* in costume.

Farfariello wrote his own music and was accompanied by his son who played on a portable piano. Later, this piano was placed on a truck and played on the streets of New York mostly for *feste* for the Italian American communities (a step higher than the itinerant Italian organ grinder). The well-chosen music and the classical were played with supreme virtuosity. Farfariello had enormous audiences in the best houses and was acclaimed in Europe and South America. There were other actors of note in the days of Italian theater, including Concetta and Edward Zacconi of Brooklyn, who were both stage and radio stars. Concetta Zacconi's sister Josephine Gambino and Eduardo her husband and their daughter Anna, also had their heyday. Other actors were Salvatore Quaranta and Clemente Gigli. There were at least a dozen film makers and distributors active in New York and the East in the 1930s and I met most of them while my husband had his own film exchange which is still at 630 9th Avenue in Manhattan.

The Italians who came to these shows included the very old and the very young. Many people from the Little Italy neighborhoods frequented the performances, although not too many of our boarders attended since they had to be in by nine o'clock.

In 1919, shortly after the end of World War I, my father decided the old neighborhood was changing and was no longer the best place to raise us. So, to my mother's chagrin, we moved up to 1634 Maple Road in what was then called S. Euclid or, simply, the Heights. Father had noticed that near the Rockefeller Estate, there was a house for sale which he now could afford since he had achieved an independent gardening route. He worked on what was popularly called "Millionaire's Row" near the Oakwood Country Club. My only brother, Anthony, caddied at the golf club there and later became its golf "pro", thereby making many contacts with rich businessmen who affected the tenor of his entire life. My brother became associated with the Cleveland Browns (football), the Zone Cab (taxis), the Guarantee Title and Trust Co., and some horse racing news publications from Ohio, although this phase of his career is not clear to me. I suspect I was purposely kept uninformed of a vast financial empire and its workings. I was a bookish "nut" from their point of view and so I knew only vaguely that some "business" and perhaps rackets were involved. I steered clear of them and, to the amazement and derision of the community and the abhorrence of my father, went off to get my formal education.

The religious services available to us during our early years were adequate. We availed ourselves only of church attendance and priests' services for special religious holidays and what I term vital statistics. That is, we were baptized soon after birth, made our First Communion after proper instruction, took on an additional name for Confirmation, were married in the Church and buried with a High Mass and/or grave rites.

Those who were not regular in church attendance were denied the glory of the central aisle for their marriages or funerals. These reprobates were ushered into the side entrance of the church for burial. The godparents for confirmees were denied the privilege of being godparents if their answers to the priest's probing sounded too liberal. Personally, I was told I was a good Christian and not a good Catholic. I had doubly sinned: once by teaching the *Parables of Jesus* at the University Baptist Church in Austin, Texas; and second by being a missionary in a black Protestant community during my freshman and sophomore years. Oh yes, and in Cleveland, Ohio, I was a Boy Scout temporary leader in 1926 (after I had obtained my Bachelor of Science degree in Education from Ohio State University). I had overheard the Italian Baptist minister complain of a lack of leadership in the community so I volunteered, was accepted and stayed on until a male was found to take over. This was interpreted as "crazy" by the neighbors. They blamed it on too much reading.

The clergy available to us were good, kind, but sometimes limited. They helped the poor, comforted the bereaved, and counseled the confused women of the community. The Irish priests in Little Italy were sometimes arrogant but largely respected. Father Francis Haley was a patient home visitor, confessor, and helper. The Trivisonos and other families mentioned in the *Church History of Holy Rosary Church* labored hard to pay off the mortgage, establish a parochial school and acquire their own social hall to offset the hated Protestant influence of their rival — the Alta House. In the early days one had to choose either the Church or the settlement house. Now, however, I understand that this schism has been healed through the valiant efforts of the enlightened Church and settlement house leaders. There was also a Protestant Church on Murray Hill Road and one later in the Collinwood, "Five Points" (spin-off of Little Italy) on Kipling Road, which numbered many Italians in their congregations.

In later years native American clergy were assigned to our parishes. They seemed more attractive than their somber Italian trained confreres. I remember getting to know one jolly younger Italian priest who had a real *joie de vivre*. Basically, it was the attitude of the older, 'ex-monks' that repelled me as a youngster.

As I look back now, I can truly say that I have lived a full life with many rich experiences. Indeed I am eager to inform people about them. I guess that is the teacher in me. In closing I should like to emphasize the love for things Italian which I have. It is, in a sense, my husband's heritage to me, to my sons, my grandchildren, and even to my non-Italian daughters-in-law.

Julian E Miranda

y paternal grandfather left the town of Castelbuono, of the province of Palermo, Sicily, near the turn of the century. Arriving in the United States he sought naturalization immediately and received his citizenship papers in 1907. He did not plan to return to Italy for reasons which stem from the reasons he left there in the first place. There was a time when my family was quite privileged, affluent and titled, but as a result of my great-grandfather's squandering through gambling, a great amount of money was lost which consequently reduced my family to a state of genteel poverty.

My grandfather, who was the oldest of two sons and three daughters, was educated by the family with great sacrifice, in the hopes that he would become a lawyer, marry well and re-establish the family fortune. Instead he was interested in the arts and wanted to be a painter, so there was conflict with his father. He then married the daughter of a cabinet-maker against his family's will which had another marriage in mind and, as a consequence of this conflict with his father and with the people of his class, he felt he could no longer remain. There was some *cavalleria rusticana* that went on, but because of the southern Italian mores, he became something of a pariah among his own class which looked down on him because he had married lower than his social standing.

Since he was a proud man, he decided to leave, initially intending to go to South America. I am sorry he did not go there because I believe we would have acclimated better to South America, since our name is Spanish, and my father was a professional man. Because of the family trouble, which remained obscure in family conversations, he was given some help in getting out of Italy. In the United States, however, there were no relations to help him, only a few *paesani* who knew him. He was a well-liked man who came to the United States in steerage and went to Ellis Island. He remembered that experience but, like most Italian immigrants, he spoke of it very little. His knowledge of the United States was very sketchy. As an intelligent man he did not expect the streets to be paved with gold, but I do not think he had any precise knowledge of what he was going to encounter.

He landed in lower Manhattan, with very little money, and was assaulted by the usual collection of thieves, crooks, *padrones* and labor contractors. He used to relate a very characteristic incident which might be regarded as apocryphal but, nevertheless, was a typical Sicilian immigrant kind of story. He was walking down lower Broadway, dressed rather well, with a cane — a real *signoré* — when a cop said something like, "Where did you get that suit, — *dago*?" My grandfather, who was very nervous after a bad ocean trip on a German ship (Hamburg Line), walked across the street and belted him with the cane. Grandpa always said he did not understand the word, but he recognized the tone. That was why he left Italy and he did not wish to put up with the same here. He was arrested and a family member was contacted who raised enough money to bribe him out.

Finding work was a problem for my grandfather because there was little work for people with his kind of education. Finally, one day he was walking and saw house painters going to work on one of the municipal buildings. He asked them whether they were in need of a painter, meaning a painter in the fine arts sense, since at that time, homes were decorated with murals, rosettas and flowers. They misunderstood and said yes, they did need a painter. He reported the next day, put on his overalls and worked there for about a year.

He had come from Italy alone and had no family with him although he had two children who remained in Italy. He shared a room with a number of other immigrants on Mulberry Bend, near Baxter Street. He then moved to Avenue A or Avenue B, which was a Sicilian quarter at that time. He began to know a few people and managed, with considerable hardship, to earn his living, saving enough money to bring his wife and two children to the United States. They then moved down to Baxter Street again where he could not get more than one room. My father was about eight at this time and he recalled that in this neighborhood there were people on the street who organized gangs. My father, who eventually became a concert pianist, was evidently very good with his hands, and he became an extremely skilled pickpocket. He had been told by this one 'Fagan', who was also Italian, that he should practice picking wallets in a jacket. One night when my grandfather saw my father at practice, he punished him severely, and was determined that, at any sacrifice, he would get out of that area. My grandfather wanted to go someplace where there would be trees. Coincidentally, at that time on Sundays he frequently would go to Central Park and paint. One Sunday a pretty WASP lady came by and asked him whether he did portraits, to which he said yes. Consequently, he painted her portrait and she introduced him to others whose portraits he painted. Meeting many wealthy people, including Italian nobility who had married into rich American families, he also met the director of the Brooklyn Institute of Arts and Sciences where he was accepted on the staff (c.1913).

After this he was able to buy a house in a non-Italian neighborhood which was significant in the development of my family. Much of our assimilation or adjustment took place then in the largely old Brooklyn kind of family neighborhood. Initially, my grandfather was not wanted there. He had a dark or olive complexion, was very proud, and determined that he was going to move there nevertheless. After he bought the house and moved he became both respected and liked.

My mother's family came to the U.S. for different reasons. They were a land owning family that had produced eleven children. They were what was called in Sicily, *Industriale,* which does not translate well into English. They had a farm and a number of businesses related to agrarian pursuits which they managed. For example, they did all the flour grinding for two or three towns in the vicinity. My mother and father had come from the same town. This is a traditional Italian pattern. My paternal grandfather, Antonio, was the godson of my maternal grandfather, and the marriage was pretty much set because it was the custom among upper middle class Sicilian families to try to marry into what they considered the aristocracy. My mother's family had very beautiful girls, but there was not enough dowry for all eleven children, nine of whom where daughters. My maternal grandfather's notion was to come to the United States, which he did in style with almost $25,000. He came to this country with the view that all peasants were fools, and all Nordics were made to be gulled. He believed he would open a business, make a lot of money, and return to Italy able to "buy" Sicily and dower all his daughters. What happened, instead, was that he was totally unequipped for the transition. What he regarded as making a living out of his innate ability to work was not the case here. He was not trained to compete in the American atmosphere. Consequently, the very people whom he regarded as *contadini* and workers, ended up, not dishonestly, owning his business. The system that had sustained him in Italy would not work here. In that system, the parent too frequently exploited the children. Grandfather sent them off to work, but gave no care for their education always with the idea that in a few years they would get back to Sicily and they would be set up with wonderful husbands and live as aristocrats. The result was that out of nine daughters, six never were married, because each time a suitor would present himself he was regarded first of all an economic threat to grandfather and, of course, he was not suitable by grandfather's standards. His daughters lived their lives in a kind of martyrdom. They might just as well never have left Sicily. None of them ever returned. I was the first in my family to return to Italy and I was the second generation. My father and mother were born there but were very young when they came to this country. In 1932 my grandfather (Miranda), was asked to return to Italy by the fascist government so he could be given an honor for some painting. My grandfather refused, however, feeling some charges may have been pending against him. He was passionately loyal to his Italian heritage and was quite parochially Sicilian.

Grandfather (Miranda) taught both me and my brother. He would come to the house twice a week with a *brichitari* (Italian A B C books). He insisted that we learn both Italian and Sicilian as two separate languages. He was mixed on this whole question since, at the turn of the century, Italy dreamed of creating a sort of French republic. It was a time of great nationalism and my grandfather had been thoroughly brainwashed with this ideal. Consequently, while he felt this general loyalty, at the same time he also felt strongly the *companilista* and was resentful of the behavior and attitudes of non-Sicilian Italians. The extent of that patriarchal influence was so great that I find I bear the mark of many of his attitudes.

For an educated man my grandfather had an unusual commitment to the Italian American community in that he started one of these *Mutuo Succorso* societies. These groups were an important institution for the early Italian Americans. He also started the *Società Nuova Nebrodesi Castelbuono*. Nebrode was the old name for the mountains, the *Madonia* mountains, in which his village was located. The society was composed of people from his home town and my grandfather was automatically elevated to the presidency. The level of literacy was not high among Italian Americans and each year there would be a kind of revolution as some would try to put him out of office. He would then refuse to run and others would come to the house and he would allow himself to be persuaded to run. He gave a tremendous amount of service, writing letters, preparing documents, etc.

There was a constant parade of people coming in and out of the house asking for help.

There was also a problem for him that was unique. As an educated man it was hard for him to find work, peers and people with whom he could pursue his interests. Consequently, he was torn with a passionate ethnicity. Italian was always spoken at home and he supported Mussolini although he despised him and criticized him among Italians. In the presence of non-Italians, Mussolini was supported by my grandfather because, after all, Mussolini was an Italian. To lead his professional life and to get that kind of stimulus in a country where there were not enough educated Italians one would have to seek it deliberately. As a result, he moved out of the neighborhood and closer to the museum near his work. At the same time he went back to his old neighborhood constantly. The Society met on Avenues A and B. He was down there two or three times a week and would play cards and do everything he could to help them.

A measure of the contribution of this Society was the service rendered by a doctor who was also a relative, and an absolute saint, Dr. Minar. Dr. Minar was no more than four feet nine. He would never take money from his patients. He survived only on payments in kind. Therefore, he had a house in which there was absolutely no money but it was filled with eggs, statues, eggplants, and sausages. He never had a nickel to his name because he could never, even when they would try to pay him, accept money because the immigrants were too poor.

Dr. Minar could be called at any hour of the night even though he never drove a car. He lived in the East Village somewhere and would get up at three in the morning and travel the BMT subway in the middle of the night for hours and arrive with his little bag. He was a brusk, terse, fast-talking man who was infinitely kind. He radiated an absolute aura of kindness. Dr. Minar was not only well-schooled but he also practiced a kind of faith healing. Nobody who was dying was told he was dying. He was always told he had a mild case of indigestion and that he should eat a good meal. Yet, he would say, "It's not really necessary but you may call the priest if you want. You will make Fr. Cottone happy."

My grandfather eventually called over his brother Paul from Italy and had a reconciliation of sorts with his father. My great-grandfather by this time was in his seventies and came here during a time of a very unusual kind of emigration. There was nothing to do for families such as mine in the old country. It was a kind of unemployment. It was a class that had outlived its usefulness. In that society you were either very, very wealthy, or you were an unemployed gentleman, and since there was absolutely nothing for the latter to do, they went to seed in spades. I am sure that that was what the gambling and all of the other escapades were about.

When my grandfather came here he lived in the East Village. An eccentric man who when he landed said to his son Paul, "Get a *carrozza;* get a carriage and drive me to the city, I want to take a look at what it is like". After looking it over he said, "Compared to an Italian city this is miserable". He never really went off the block for the next twenty years. He had only one friend and he was Chinese.

I always remember, however, that a strong sense of hardship survived in the family. For example, when his family lived on Baxter Street my father had a brother who was ill with pneumonia. At the time there was no doctor here that my grandfather knew well and there was so little money that my grandfather was unable to get a doctor for the child. He went to American hospital authorities who were totally indifferent and the child died. My father remembers the heartbreaking picture of my grandfather making the coffin for his son, decorating it and holding the small coffin on his knees as the carriage journeyed out to Long Island where he dug a deep hole, said a service and buried the child.

By getting out of the neighborhood, the family was afforded none of the protections that the ethnic Italian neighborhood gave you but, at the same time, the family found itself able to function more quickly out of necessity. I think that had there not been some level of education they would not have been able to do this. Being literate in Italian, knowing a little French and English, and having a profession, my father found social acceptance. He would not have found the same without this background. He dared to leave the protection of the neighborhood but he was in the position to dare.

My father, who was a concert pianist, bought a house outside of the Italian area because he realized there was no money to be earned in the Italian neighborhood teaching piano to children of Italian immigrants who didn't have any money. They were willing to pay only ten cents a lesson, which reflects the value they placed on his talent. It is my impression that Italians are extremely unmusical despite their reputation. I have known very few Italians who sang in choral groups or played music at home. They did like dancing but not really folk dancing as for example, did the Poles or Ukrainians. Thus, when my father bought his house he was told exactly the same thing told to my grandfather and also told me in my neighborhood,

"We don't want too many of your kind here". In all the time I grew up in this WASP neighborhood I can never recall being invited into anybody's home despite the fact my father was quite the item. He subsequently became the chairman of the music department in his high school. Everyone was always polite, very genteel, but there was always some fear that we might miscegenate. This did teach me something very important. That is, the discrimination against Italians was not a matter of social class, but was, in fact, an ethnic or racial discrimination. It did not really matter what class you came from.

The Italians grew up under a delusion that if somehow we all got educated and learned the American language and American ways of life, discrimination would be ended. This was not the case. In that neighborhood when the kids got mad at me I was a "guinea". This concept was central to my development as an individual and is one of the reasons why I entered the civil rights movement for blacks and Puerto Ricans. It is also one of the reasons I became involved in the Italian movement. Had I been convinced that it was a matter of education for economic success rather than education for psychological self-acceptance, I would have been less a protestor and more of a scholar. It has been an unusual experience.

On the topic of the church, it must be remembered that Southern Italian men were not so church scrupulous as the women although they were Catholic. I think no one should mistake their non-church attendance for a lack of belief in the Roman Catholic faith. The seeming lack of scrupulosity in Italians should not delude anybody about their lack of commitment to Christianity and its central ideas. I think there is a great paradox, and a great ambivalence there. Basically they dislike the clergy, and if they dislike the Italian clergy they despise the American clergy. They were very cruelly treated by this group. I remember when I was a child going for my First Communion and, I was asked by one of the nuns to recite the Our Father. I had only known it in either Sicilian or Latin (dog Latin). I knew what was going to happen but I got up and recited it and of course the class guffawed and the nun made fun of me. In a rage, I left the class. It was a Sunday and my grandfather was coming to the house, saw my face and said *che succedio?* (what happened?). At first, I did not want to tell him because of the *omerta* (you did not whine) but I finally told him that I said my prayer in Sicilian and they laughed at me. Inside of thirty seconds he had me by the arm and had propelled me up to the church. There, he got hold of Fr. Fitzsimmons and the nun and verbally laid them out. Nevertheless, this affected my church attendance. The lack of concern by the church for the immigrants and the cultural difference between the Italian and Irish Catholicism was responsible for a lot of the movement of Italians out of the Church toward Protestantism. This was also, however, a way to upward mobility. Had there been Italian clergy there is no question but that it would have made a difference. First of all the mere fact of being able to converse with the priest in your own language is important, but the role of the priest has been limited until very recently. The priest was not really a social agent by and large. I do not think priests gave social assistance beyond the performance of their strictly religious functions.

I have spent much time assessing myself in this period and I have tried to locate the key points that made myself and my family somewhat different from may Italian immigrants. I think the key was leaving the neighborhood more than anything else. People of the same kind of background from my own town and even my own family who remained in the Italian neighborhood have experienced greater cultural conflict and are much more inhibited by the culture. I think that the Italian family has been far from a benign influence on the Italian American. I have known of many disruptive influences and not because of any evil intentions. As Covello writes, the family was designed to function as a patriarchial unit with everybody responding to the needs of the family rather than to his individual needs. A great deal of our lack of social mobility is because psychologically we are unable to tear ourselves away from our family ties, and because so few of us within a given family are formally educated. Therefore, because we so love our family and we are so committed to it we lead a great deal of our social life still at the urban villager level. With other groups, which have been here longer, or in which the family pattern is not so restrictive or who tend to move out of the ethnic neighborhoods, one is more inclined to seek peers from one's work life. This is a great assistance to the immigrant both materially and intellectually. Of course, the beautiful part of family life is then lost.

When I was studying human relations at New York University there was a great deal spoken about the lack of social mobility and occupational mobility among Italians and I was constantly in conflict with those who contended this. I tried to make them see that from my Italian American vantage-point our value system contained much wisdom. Success is measured in terms of whether a person got what he wanted. The Italian immigrant came for very definite reasons, not one of which he has not accomplished. He came here for economic security, economic advancement, and escape from the hopelessness of the old country. He wanted a

decent life with decent material things which would lessen the tensions of
the family and he did it. Italians are working in the lower middle class, but
there is a relatively low rate of mental dysfunction among them. There is
certainly now a very low crime rate. They still tend to some degree to
ghettoize but I think that is going to disappear very rapidly (which may not
not be good) as cities disintegrate. I have no quarrel with the "melting pot"
concept. I think it contains a good objective: the development of a people
through the free evolution of all peoples to society, and the evolution of a
constantly dynamic answer to what America is. This is the only answer to
the attainment of peoplehood. I think we presently suffer from the lack of
peoplehood. What I have objected to is the value judgments made upon
what cultures shall contribute; the enforced shucking of values, the enforced
homogenization; and the arrogant decisions by some elements in society
that their way shall be *the* way and that we are good or bad depending on
the degree to which we imitate them.

During World War II, two of my uncles returned to Italy voluntarily to
serve in the Italian army. We had a very large family on my mother's side
in Italy and many of them served. They had strong sympathies for Italy and
remained nationalistic once over here. World War II was, for those
members of my family who were Italian born and Italian raised, a traumatic
experience. They were frightened, fearing they might be interned. They
had no political loyalty toward Italy but they were still torn. I know I was.

When I went into the army it was a heartbreaking experience, I specifically
requested not to go to Italy. I had relatives there. This is an affirmation of
the persistence of the culture. Remember, my grandfather came here in
his late twenties and, my father was only seven or eight. My mother was
about fourteen or fifteen and we did not grow up in an Italian neighborhood.
Yet, I grew up knowing how to speak Sicilian with such an intimate
knowledge of the Sicilian town and all of the inter-relations of the family,
that I could, as I indeed did, go to the town and walk through it as if I had
lived there. I knew them but they did not know me. If there had been only
one war, either war with Europe, or with Italy, I would have accepted the
assignment to the best of my ability. I felt an aversion to the fascist
government and a deep loyalty to the United States. Granted the choice,
however, and the fact that there were other fronts, I realized that it would
be abrasive to fight against Italy. My cousin actually fought in Sicily and
went through his family's home town. I would have found this very
difficult to do and I am sure I would have been in trouble with the army. In
fact, I was in trouble on occasion because I fraternized with Italian

prisoners and this was poorly looked upon.

This occurred in Missouri where I hung around the prison camp because I was trying to find something of home. I wanted to hear the language. Although my father and mother spoke some Sicilian, there was less and less of it. I was homesick and the sound of the language, the smell of the food, and seeing those faces got to me. They seemed closer to me than the people downtown. I felt more affinity to the prisoners of war than I felt to the Tennessean and Floridian. Finally, I was confined to quarters for visiting them and they came to see me. We had some uproarious times laughing about the irony of the situation since I was an American soldier and I was confined. Yet they were prisoners of war and they could come and visit me. They brought me salami. I was very conflicted about the Italian performance in the war, in an immature way. I wanted them to fight and hold their ground, but I didn't want them to fight and hold their ground because it was my country they were fighting. It was a cause of great concern for me. Before I went into the army the thought of it almost made me ill. All my life I had been raised on stories about these people and it hurt me deeply to fight them. I grew to hate Mussolini who brought me to this dilemma. It would have been very difficult for me to shell an Italian town, especially a Sicilian town.

The Italian American population was not split at all regarding Mussolini. They upheld support for the Italian government, regardless of who was ruling. It could have been Attila the Hun, or it could have been the Pope. This was the first time that they had seen Italy as a nation achieve something which, in their view, was commensurate with what other governments were achieving. Almost all of the Italians I knew supported the government. Most of them were probably monarchists. All the people I knew in the Italian radio seemed to be. My grandmother gave her gold ring and I think she no more had an idea about fascism than she did of any other political systems. The popular view of fascism was a naive one. Finally, someone had come along to make Italians do what they were supposed to do and the English world seemed to respect them.

There was considerable church propaganda also because there was a feeling that fascism was combatting communism which was concerned with the destruction of Christianity. I think their main perceptions were, "now they have to respect us". The Italians felt so denigrated in this country that it gave them some pride when Italo Balbo came over, or Italian battleships visited. Italian Americans wanted Italy to be on a par with America as a world power. Most Italians felt and still feel that Italians need a strong hand, and that the only way to make them do what they are supposed to do is to force them. I think that comes because the sole institution is the family and that Italians just do not function as Americans do in reference to government. They do not look to government as the solution to their problems. Consequently, governments in Italy have a hard time justifying their existence. I found no dichotomy. I went to a rally with my grandfather in 1935 in support of the Abbysinian War. My grandfather fought in the first Abbysinian War and he hated having fought in it. Thinking the war was an injustice to both sides and abhorring the ludicrous and imperialistic generals he, nevertheless, went to this rally because it was an Italian thing. It was like criticizing your father. You just do not do that publicly.

I had grown up with some knowledge of the Italian language which was far from perfect so I studied it further in college. I thought all Italians were artists. This, of course was an entirely unrealistic picture I drew because of the neighborhood in which I grew up, and because everybody in my family was a musician and very gifted. I had not seen their mortality at all. After graduating from college I began to look for work in radio. Yet, because of the intense discrimination and the fact that the only place where I would be accepted was in an Italian American radio station, I went to work as a censor. This position was called editor but really was a censor. During the war all the broadcasts that were put on the air in Italian had to be read first by me for propaganda and obscenity, although it was the propaganda they were concerned with. After this I began doing bit parts in Italian theater for fun and I acted in some of the radio dramas. I found Italian theater hilariously funny and a great deal of fun. Italian American radio theater played a tremendous part in the lives of Italian Americans for a period of about fifteen years from about 1932 or 1933 until the end of World War II. By 1950 it was virtually dead.

Among the several reasons for the phenomenal growth of Italian American radio in the 1930s were, first of all, the decline of the silent film. During the era of silent film the immigrant could go to the movies of all ethnic groups and the pictures carried the story. At that time when you went to the movies you would hear Yiddish, Italian or Polish, as everybody was explaining what was happening on the screen. The pictures were combined so that one could do this. Then, when the talkies began, since many of the immigrants could not follow the words they ceased attending. At this time commercial radio had reached its full development. Consequently, a group of people formed fifteen Italian theater companies which somewhat paralleled the peripatetic circuses and theater companies which had thrived in Italy. The people who gravitated toward these companies were not always actors by trade but were generally people who could read. There was also a regional theater that was going on in addition to the theater in the Italian languages. In other words, there was a Neapolitan theater company which put on the traditional kind of Neapolitan drama.

In a typical Neapolitan play there would be two stark characters, not columbine necessarily, but their origins were manifest. These stock characters would be confronted with a given situation, one of them would throw out a line, the other would pick out a line and then they would extemporize a comedy routine in the dialect. There were some famous Italian American actors who did this. The descendent of one of the luminaries of this Italian American theater is Vincent Gardenia, whose father started a theater on Canal Street and ran many theatrical companies. In addition, there were many Sicilian companies who specialized in classic Sicilian dramas. These were very different kinds of stories and very expressive of the difference in culture. For example, the themes in Sicilian drama are the themes of honor, romance and revenge. They are the stark gothic stories *Verga* and *Capabuono* and *Cavalleria Rusticana* and these were then performed in Sicilian. The artist among these was a man named il Cav. Rosario Romeo, who had been knighted. There was also a fine Sicilian dramatist named Pirandello. There was a good Sicilian literature at this time too, as there was a fine Neapolitan literature which was satirical, or sometimes romantic but its specialty was satirical literature.

Giorgio Campobasso, who is dead now, produced a number of stories about turn-of-the century Naples. These were picturesque stories about characters who lived by their ingenuity outwitting the Bourbon police.

Basically, the number of companies was in direct relation to the number of people who came from the region. So while there were no Apugliese companies, there were Apugliese comedians. They, too, expressed something in the Apugliese ethos which is an earthy, materialistic and satirical commentary on the human soul. In fact, there was one famous man named Michele Raponaro Mingucho Barrese (Little Mike). He had a famous skit having to do with a very beautiful widow whose husband has died and her brother-in-law who is at the funeral. It is called "The Consolation of the Widow", and it is a little Boccaccian. He starts out comforting her with his arm around her and pretty soon they disappear into the shrubbery.

They also did many religious dramas in Italian. In the eastern quadrant going up into Toronto, wherever there were Italians, there were companies which travelled and performed. These were companies of twenty to thirty people who travelled and performed these Italian dramas in the Italian neighborhoods. This movement may be paralleled to the production of many of the same dramas on the Italian radio stations. Often, people would listen to the episodes on the radio and then go to see the play. When you went to see the plays you would see shows that went on for three or four hours. These plays might have twenty or twenty-five acts with some of the best acting or the worst acting that the human race has ever seen. There were singers, and there was always a Neapolitan singer (probably a classic Neapolitan singer) then there was a Sicilian singer who did stark kinds of folk songs and then there were the off-color songs. It was a kind of dramatic relief.

Here also was an occasion where the people could talk about and see publicly racey stories despite the restrictive Italian mores. It was all done in parables. Perhaps you remember this one: *"Che se mangiato la zita la prima sera?"* (What did the bridegroom have with him the first night? A sausage, a cucumber and two oranges). Many of these were very Boccaccian or Rabelaisian, and very medieval. These companies also had some remarkable casts.

There was a man named Sterni, who had been Commandatore Sterni, having been honored by the Italian government. He did very well and was a very literate man. There was also Rosario Romeo who was a friend of Pirandello and a superb actor. There was *Farfariello* who was an international actor, the Cantinflas of Italy and a genius. Yet, there seemed to be less transfer of Italian actors and Italian theater to America than there was in the Jewish theater, for example. Perhaps this was because the Italians were not so interested in theater in the abstract as the Jews were. Also the Italians were not so literate as the Jews and, by and large, the former did not have the leads into the show-business community, which enabled so many Jewish actors to cross over into the American theater. Only a few of the Italian actors were able to do this. I knew many of them such as the Miniciotti family who played Hollywood Italian mothers and fathers. Esther Minciotti is one of my closest friends. Her husband was a descendant of performers from Italy. I also know an old man who was a tumbler and a descendant of a tumbling family in Italy. They had a unique society in which they all knew each other.

The Italian broadcasting went from 9:00 in the morning to 6:00 at night. The shows were generally half-hour shows with some fifteen minute shows. From this schedule alone one can see how many shows and how many companies were involved. The men who ran these companies earned a substantial amount of money. There were occasions when mounted police had to be called out to control the crowds. They would mob the actors afterwards because they were so realistic. Once in New York I remember seeing a man called Gino Caini playing St. Francis and people rushed backstage to kiss the hem of his robe.

Some of the theaters in which Italian plays were put on were the Academy of Music and the Polish American Labor Federation, since they played in a lot of union halls. There were also theaters in Bushwick, Brooklyn and on Tremont Avenue in the Bronx. I was a lousy actor and in my young twenties took a somewhat laughing view of the whole thing. My friends and I clowned our way through, to the despair of those who ran the companies. After all, this was an important part of their lives and a source of great economic benefit to many Italian manufacturers. An Italian advertising industry grew up out of the theater alone. Products like Paramount Macaroni, La Rosa, Medaglia d'Oro Coffee, flourished, as did the olive oil companies because they were associated with radio advertising. That industry died as Italian radio died. Guilio Amali played Pasquale C.O.D. (Cash on Delivery). I knew him very well. I was regarded kind of laughingly as a young pup whose antics were to be tolerated as a young but good enough actor — or at least Italian.

I worked at the WOV radio station for two and a half years starting in 1942 while I was still in college. When I went into the army they held my job for me. When I got out of the army I went back to work for them for a year and a half. This was my start in the media. I left the station because I thought the world was my oyster and I was going to go on to American radio. We did not make it. I remember going to Young and Rubican in 1945, a company in which my uncle was a major stockholder. Despite this I was given the shuffle. They were willing to buy my material blind but they were unwilling to put me on the staff.

One of the men called me into his office and closed the door saying, "Look let me level with you. You're Italian and I'm Italian. My name is not Adams it's Adanti. You will never get into any of these companies unless you change your name." I struck a pose and drew my sword and said, "Never! On this ground I stand."

The Italian audience alone could not support those of us who wanted to get into these fields. The Jews on the other hand bought their own agencies and whatever institutions they were not allowed into, they took control and formed on their own. We had neither the resources nor the inclinations to do this and, as a result, many of us perished. Only now are some Italians breaking into the media. If you notice on television most or many of the technicians are Italian, although few producers bear Italian names.

Some of the actors, however, did make it. Gardenia remains a lovely fellow. He is still very available. He took his success beautifully, as befitting a lovely Neapolitan man.

I knew Generoso Pope very slightly although I did know his sons. I felt they were exploiting the Italian American community running their empire like Renaissance dukes, with sycophants and intrigue. I think, by and large, the Pope family was a good thing for the Italian American community, but they were not good for me. I was unwilling to genuflect.

Radio was tremendously important for Italians, and there were many well known people involved, such as Luigi Antonini, or *l'avvocato* (the lawyer), Lupis. I remember once meeting Carlo Sforza when he was under a pseudonym although I forget what he called himself. Generoso Pope's radio station was a poor level of radio. By contrast, WHOM was a much more universal radio station because it was not run by Italians and therefore, did not advocate one point or view or another. WHOM was owned by the Bulova Watch Company and nobody in a key position was Italian. As such, the points of view that were expressed were neither pro-fascist nor anti-fascist. Their news coverage was very good, and they could be credited with pretty good public service broadcasting. Considering the level of literacy of most of the audience, some of the radio programs were really very good. Sincere attempts were made to provide good entertainment although mostly, it was melodrama. They plagiarized incredibly. Some of the shellac records were made from these broadcasts and, if they are still around today they would probably be in private collections. These records were often brought out and played at parties. I have often wanted to do a piece for the *New York Times* on "What Ever Happened to Baby Gina" or "What Ever Happened to the Italian American Theater?"

The radio performers also had a union which was called the Italian Actors Union. The Union eventually managed to get the actors $2.00 an episode. Before that they received maybe a quarter an episode or simply performed for free for the participation. In fact, sometimes the actors were even requested to kick back the two bucks. The Union had an office on 56th Street and 6th Avenue. Sometimes the International Ladies Garment Workers Union would come up with Luigi Antonini as a speaker. The trouble with the Italian leadership, especially the liberal leadership, was, however, that they tried to speak to the Italian public in what was frequently poor Italian. In addition, they harangued. People like LaGuardia spoke abominable Italian. Did you know this? LaGuardia was basically viewed as a betrayer by Italian Americans since he was not a Roman Catholic and his wife was not Italian. He also was used as a tool. Italian Americans did not like his anti-fascism. They felt he was disloyal. He had a right to be anti-fascist but not publicly.

The degree to which Italians identified with fascism was a function of two things. One was their sense of homesickness and loyalty to their own ethnic group. Second was the function of their poor self-image in this country. Except for real doctrinaire nuts, and there were very few in this country, I think most fascists were created by American prejudice and bigotry. I think that this is very different from whatever German commitment there was. If you had suggested to any of the Italians that I ever knew that Italy should conquer the United States, I think they would have hanged you, and not in effigy. I think Italians have loved this country passionately and often unrequitedly. Despite anything that was ever done to them here, this love persists. They came because they could not survive. What is it that Foerster said, *"Ubi pane, ubi patria"* (Where the bread is, that's the fatherland). They ate here and they thrived and there was hope. In the sense in which they wanted to make it here, they made it. In 2,000 years of Italian history they had never made it. I hear some of the old Italian men still saying, "My grandson is two heads and a half taller than I am — from the same blood! Why? Because he was fertilized by good food."

In the field of professional education, discrimination was and has been acute. It sometimes was covert and sometimes even unconscious. I think it has been quite acute. I remember one time wanting to enter the foreign service and sending away for the applications. The forms requested country of origin, birthplace of parents, etc. Later, I was informally told by people in the organization that any one with a "foreign" background would have little hope of being accepted.

I also remember a low level of expectation from my teachers, which actually amazed me. I went to Samuel J. Tilden High School where my father was a teacher, after which I attended Brooklyn College, Columbia University and then New York University where I received my Master's. I found the message was always the same at one level or another: "You are a bright guy and very articulate and very a-typical".

Because of the fields I was interested in I also found great difficulty finding work. I did not want to do menial work. In the forties I was sending letters and applications to jobs for which I was eminently qualified. I probably completed over 1,000 to which I never received an answer. I was told quite bluntly by one of the major banks on Wall Street that they were not hiring anyone but Ivy League, which meant no Italians or Jews, quite obviously. There was also discrimination in the State Education Department. I spent 19 and a half years there and I did not know of three administrators who were Italian. There never was an Italian American commissioner or assistant commissioner. I knew only three Italian bureau chiefs that I can remember and one of them had changed his name. I worked in the field of race relations, human rights and civil rights and I constantly found Italian Americans described as backward and uneducated because of their lack of interest in education.

Never was there anything lacking in the system, yet I found it very difficult to find schools that taught Italian. I found that the knowledge of the Italian language was not a respected knowledge within the schools. My father went to the Board of Education and took the test to become a music teacher. He was told the same thing I've heard all my life, "Tony, you know we don't want too many Italians. They have an attitude toward music that's rather operatic." My father had trouble passing his piano test and yet he had been called by Paderewski, "the young Italian American Paderewski".

I have met discrimination in the media. I have had many people think that they were flattering me by expressing amazement at my attainment which they would have easily accepted with other groups. The head of the Human Relations Bureau of the State Education Department one day asked me whether I wasn't unduly sensitive about the whole business of the Italian American underworld. Is it not possible that, not from anything genetic, but through historical, cultural circumstances and oppression that southern Italians may have more of an affinity or propensity for crime? I replied that he would not have said this about another group. By that test, I said, "Wouldn't you Norwegians and Scandinavians have a propensity for rape, pillage and burning?"

Many members of my family belonged to labor unions. My grandfather's brother was very active. Calling himself an anarchist, he even fought the Pinkertons in Union Square. He was so badly beaten by them that he had six hernias, and was permanently disabled all his life. My mother worked for a time in the garment business and joined the union movement with other Italian women even though they did not totally understand what it was about since they were largely illiterate. Socialist and anarchist groups among the Italian Americans were also active but not influential. They were of the Sacco and Vanzetti kind. I mean this in the sense that they were isolated and many had sympathy for them, largely a sympathy because they were Italian. I think one of the traumas of the Italian American experience has been the Sacco and Vanzetti matter. I think there are certain things that have happened to us that we forget much as we forget childhood traumas, that have left their mark upon us. I think the New Orleans lynching was another of these incidents which touched them and angered them. The same for the Sacco-Vanzetti case. It was constantly discussed by all Italian Americans, and it was viewed as an anti-Italian act. Still, it did not recruit anarchists and socialists.

I also remember being angry that there were no Italian priests. Yet, we were probably angrier with those Italian priests here. The Italians felt that it was an alien church, and the Irish were very cruel to them. I believe that much of the ecumenical movement, is an anti-ethnic movement. I think it is part of the elitist repudiation on the part of Irish and German leadership versus the Polish, Italian and middle European Catholics. I do not think it is that clear-cut but I do find it ironic that Italians were criticized for their lack of scrupulosity when I was a kid, and that they are now criticized for their over-scrupulosity. That makes one wonder. The absence of Italian clergy is not just a struggle over celibacy. There has to be a hegemony exercised. I consider myself a Catholic, a traditional, conservative Catholic. I was a liberal Catholic until the ecumenical movement came. I think there is a lot of anti-Italianism in it. I think that we are being robbed of a cultural institution which is very, very important. The removal of Latin from the Mass is another act of deculturalization. I do not like the American church. I like to look at the Italian church. I like the Italian church visually, operatically, historically, theatrically and culturally and because I feel it is a big institution which we control. I also do not like the Nordic Catholicism which holds the sense of a strict adherence to rules where the only hope of changing Catholicism is to change the rules. We change them ourselves whenever we want to informally, and this is much more human. Pope is pop and in public you did not criticize him. I think in essence that is much more practical. Nordics do not understand this language. Barzini would understand. If the transgression is not too bad, it is much better to me, if your kids sneak around the corner, then tell you "Drop dead Pop, I'm not going to do what you say." Then, you have lost your authority completely. Catholicism by nature has to be authoritarian. If Catholicism isn't Roman I lose a lot of interest. I'm very chauvinistic. Grandpa did a good job.

Regarding Italian American politics, I certainly remember that the Democratic party proselytized extensively among Italians giving out favors liberally and providing an informal access to the bureaucracy. It is the loss of that among other things which has alienated Italian Americans from the Democratic party.

My father's recollection of the schools as a young Italian immigrant was very harsh. He felt that while some of the teachers were committed and kind, they were also uncomprehending. He suffered a great social stigma because he spoke broken English; so much so that in later years he learned it perfectly from records. He spoke it far less foreignly than I do. My brother was so abrased by discrimination against Italians that he went into elementary schools knowing only Italian and refused to answer a word of English. I have seen him stutter and gasp when under pressure to speak English. He really cannot speak English that well.

The existence of the Mafia in Italy is in the folklore of my family. We came from western Sicily. Schiavo noted that there is no mafia in Castlebuono. He did observe, however, that there were brigands there and mafia in other towns. There is no question that in my grandfathers', my mother's father's business there was a mafia extortion carried on. This was also a recourse or a law-enforcer and very much like Puzo's Godfather, but much milder. Everyone in my mother's family, because they were in business, knew somebody. My father's family had absolutely no contact with the mafia, although I have seen it in operation. I have been in the pastry shops that they have handled and I have seen them come in with all their elaborate courtesy and ceremony and sit down and have their coffee. As a matter of fact, they helped my mother's father very much when he was threatened by another mafia family. They were very courtly, stately people and beautifully dressed. Not at all as they were depicted by Americans.

I am also of the opinion that there is no real resurgence in Italian ethnicity, although it is my belief that when the consciousness was very strong in the sixties, it was because of the activity of the blacks, Puerto Ricans and Jews. I think this level of ethnicity is not really important to Italian Americans and I think Novak is wasting his time in attempting to organize. I am very glad that the American Italian Historical Association is writing and collecting and commenting and codifying, because there may come a time when it will be of great value to know the experience of these various immigrant groups, I do think, however, that the Italians will be assimilated completely in a relatively short time. They already have very little sense of ethnicity except at a conversation or dietary level. I think they will intermarry extensively and the decline of the cities will break up the ethnic neighborhoods. The greater mobility which is ever-intruding upon our lives, scattering the families, will change the mores and Italians will enter the mainstream of American life much as the Germans did, simplifying the spelling of their names, if not actually changing them. I am no longer sorry about this because, as an American, I believe we have to have a kind of shared culture. I think the ability to remedy almost any urban situation is immediately paralyzed by the diversity of attitudes sincerely expressed by contending groups. There is, then, no way of accomplishing anything because there are so many contending groups, any one of which can prevent the power structure from deciding anything.

There is also an unwillingness to maintain pluralism and the only way we can solve our problem and achieve a peoplehood in the broader sense is by becoming American. I do not find anything at all wrong with this. What I do find wrong is people who are ashamed of being Italian and who leave the group because they are ashamed and beaten. Anyone who ceases to be Italian because he no longer wants to be Italian freely, is free to leave as far as I'm concerned. My name is Miranda and I would never change it, but if someone wishes to change his name, it does not bother me. What does bother me is when he changes it because everybody calls him a *guinea* and he is ashamed. I do not think the Italian Americans will ever visibly contribute so much to American life as some other ethnic groups. I believe that we are deculturated and that we are in some sort of nebulous limbo where what we are holding onto in the Italian culture is anything but what is important to a central ideology. We have a few mannerisms, speech patterns, foods, and something of the closed family pattern, but the essential attitudes towards life which is Italian is no longer present in the second and third generation children and they should not hang on to something that is unreal. It is valuable to me and it is precious to me because it helped to shape me. I would never give it up and I would want everybody to be free to have it. I do not, however, see the Italians joining and organizing. They do not see themselves really as an ethnic group, and indeed, resent their categorizers. No Italian book written by anybody about Italians except for *The Godfather* has ever achieved any concurrence. To publish for Italian Americans is to cry out in the wilderness. I think the movement has been perverted and exploited by politicians and self-seeking people. I went into it ideally, fanatically, and perhaps stupidly. I think it is ironic that of all the people who went into it seven or eight years ago, certainly I was one of the most vocal. Yet, none of the Italian American community has ever asked or wanted me involved in anything that it did. I think that shows that something I thought I was saying for them, I really was not saying for them, but for me. I can ask forgiveness for my arrogance. I think Italians want to be Americans as soon as possible and, some of us (including me), have been making fun of that.

I once asked Gambino how many Italian American students were taking Italian American studies at Queens College. He did not answer me. Now Gambino is capable of very precise answers. I have never been able to find out with any degree of certainty, how many Italian American students are taking Italian American studies and I think we may be forcing it. Bilingualism has been distorted for Italian Americans in attempts to create various little empires. I have been a strong advocate of bilingualism, when there is no English, as a road to acclimation and adjustment to the United States. Any attempt, however, to reorganize goes nowhere. I was with the Howard Samuels committee (when he setup an Italian American research committee) when he sought to gain nomination for governor. Some of us forged a weapon with which we hoped to gain leverage for the Italian American communities which were neglected and victimized. I took the Goldberg debacle, and pointed out what happens when you run that kind of ticket without a representation from the most numerous white ethnic group in New York State. I was one of the guys who told this to various politicians, yet I only half believed this. I wanted to believe it. The outcome was the creation of this Samuels committee whose objective was to court the Italian American bloc of voters. Yet, the Italian Americans were totally unresponsive. They would rather vote against blacks than for Italians.

From the standpoint of who represents what causes in society and whether they threaten you there is something to be said for that position.

One of the reasons Italian Americans do not vote in a bloc is that those who have purported to advocate their cause usually turn untrustworthy. What happened in the past was that the Democratic party attempted to enlist a constituency of upper class WASPS, blacks, Jews, and assorted peoples, to force them on an all or nothing basis upon Italians. They made it so unpalatable in the Lindsay years that they threw away the working class constituency. Generally I think Carter has a good chance with Italians. If he keeps talking about God enough he may do it. I also think they tend to vote for their reference image. In other words, they vote for the guy whom they secretly admire and the guy whom they secretly admire still looks a hell of a lot more like a Nordic Republican. Olive is still not beautiful to them, black is not beautiful, but the blond, blue-eyed image, they eat up. I understand this because it started in Italy. I think they will vote Republican again and against their self-interest. I think they are voting against blacks and Puerto Ricans, and in some ways for excellent reasons. There is no question that we, as a social class, have been called upon to pay that bill. They do not recognize that the Italians have been thrust into better positions in New York City by virtue of not being black and Puerto Rican. Also, in voting against the blacks, there is somebody that they are better than in the eyes of this power structure.

Since its inception in city educational institutions, open enrollment has resulted in larger numbers of Italian Americans going to city colleges. Its cut-back will probably also stop many from going to college. I would have to see figures on how many open enrollment students complete college to give an evaluation of how valuable the experience of going to City College is now as opposed to years ago. It must be evaluated in terms of what it can produce for you in life. I am torn now because I ran what is now called open enrollment for blacks a number of years ago. The early results were dubious. In the program in which I was involved we spent some 16 million dollars and I do not think that five students completed the course. That is an unthrifty expenditure of money as opposed to changing our attitudes toward occupational education. We should be taking a close look at higher education for working class people *vis-à-vis* how productive it is for them. I also wonder whether we should be taking a number of crafts and skills and elevating them above the non-professional level.

We no longer have a class of educated craftsmen, and we have lost a valuable resource. Since World War II we have been sold a bill of goods regarding education. We had better take a look at that because we are producing a lot of disoriented college graduates. Italian Americans have been unskillfully handled in the educational system. It has always been a middle class outlook that has predominated in education. They never really looked at the way our families are put together, our mores or our values.

Covello's book is the finest study on Italian Americans, although I disagree with a number of things he says. If it had been written about any other group it would be considered a classic in sociology. Yet, few who purport to be experts in the field have bothered to sit down and read his book.

Gambino's book is read. I respect Gambino but I think his book is fatuous. I hesitate to say that because I write and people comment about me. I believe I could have written that book but I chose not to. I presently have a contract for a book which I could not write because what I have to say would not be accepted by Italian Americans. I would only hurt them and make them hate me. I would nevertheless, like to study the family. I think that is something we have to look at much more closely, including the negative aspects. You cannot do this, however, with Italian Americans. You can only praise them. You can only tell them that William Paca was an Italian American, which he wasn't.

The problem for us is to recognize the nature of our prominence, to look at it objectively and clinically. There is nothing to be ashamed of in poverty, oppression, deprivation, and as Booker T. Washington pointed out, in some ways the blacks had it made compared to us. We must say that there was something extraordinary about the skills it took to survive and to adjust and manage to thread away from this morass and get as far as we did. This is a phenomenal achievement. Rather, they want it to look like something else. The achievement is that when everything is against you and you survive; but without saying that everything was against you, you cannot boast of that achievement.

There is much to be proud in the story of these poor immigrants. We did not have the kind of success the Jews had and we do not look like WASPS. It is as Barzini says, despite the fact that Italians reject his book. No, they want William Paca, whose grandfather came to England with no indication that he was Italian American. He married Oliver Cromwell's sister and you can imagine how Italian he was, since Cromwell hated Italians. But, because his name ended in a vowel they want Paca. They can have him. I have my father, your father, my wife's father and other people I know. I have better heroes.

~FIVE ~

The Social Worker
and
The Soldier

Introduction

   Americans of Italian descent have entered into a variety of fields and professions, some of which may seem atypical in comparison to the more stereotypical image of Italians as ditch diggers, barbers and seamstresses. In truth, most Italian immigrants did enter the unskilled or semiskilled occupations. Many of the children, however, entered other professions which went far beyond those of their immigrant parents.

   One of the fields in which few Italians became involved during the era of mass immigration was that of social work. Indeed, at that time, it was a largely unknown field and perhaps even suspect by immigrants. For these reasons and many others the family of Angela Carlozzi-Rossi, the daughter of immigrants from Foggia, Italy, did not react with enthusiasm when she announced she wanted to enter social work.

   Angela Carlozzi-Rossi performed as a social worker for many years, utilizing her Italian background as she assisted various and numerous people. Particularly important was her role as executive secretary of the **Italian Welfare League,** *a post she held for thirty-eight years. She also worked for twenty years as secretary-treasurer of the Welfare Photo Studio. As a result of this extensive experience she became one of the most experienced Americans of Italian descent in the field of immigration and naturalization. After several years as a social worker in Philadelphia's settlement houses, she assumed a position with the Italian Welfare League during which time she played an important role in aiding Italian immigrants who had fallen into difficulties over violations of, or misunderstandings in American immigration laws.*

The story of Angela reveals much about the problems and complications regarding immigration laws confronted by tens of thousands of Italian immigrants and their families. Even beyond this, however, her story demonstrates an early example of professional careerism among Italian American women.

It is estimated that the actual number of Italian Americans who served in the American armed services during World War II proportionately exceeded their percentages in the total population. Trying to overcome the stigma of association with an "enemy" nation Italian Americans boasted of their commitment to the war effort. Italian American neighborhoods were distinguished by the stars hanging in the windows — visible evidence of the number of Italian American young men serving in the nation's services. Although uncomfortable about engaging in war against Italy, these parents were generally proud of the opportunity to indicate their loyalty to their adopted land by the devotion of their sons to the war effort. Many of the young men distinguished themselves in combat and won numerous wartime citations.

The story of Frank J. Tarallo is a fascinating saga of the son of Italian immigrants who came to play a significant role in a little known but important chapter in the military history of World War II. Curiously, Americans are now more likely to advert to the alleged cooperation between the American Mafia, especially in the person of Lucky Luciano, and the American military forces, as the Allies prepared for the invasions of Sicily and Italy, than they are to the Italian Americans not connected with criminal activities who played an extremely important part in this military effort. As a principle participant in these operations Tarallo was in a responsible position and is thus able to reveal much about the impact of his ethnic background on wartime activity. A man of impeccable honesty and humility, I came to know Tarallo in 1975 and have maintained a warm relationship with him since. His autobiography here unfolds much about the interplay of culture and family on the one hand, and about intelligence and military operations on the other.

Angela Carlozzi-Rossi

My parents were born in Foggia, Italy, but were married in the United States about 80 years ago. They reared a large family of nine children which, with father and mother and two grandmothers, one Catholic and one Protestant, made thirteen. I was born in New York City and, like my father, was a Baptist. Although our household was crowded we got along very well. As I grew up I decided I wanted to be a nurse but my father was not happy with the idea, fearing that as a nurse I would see many things I had not seen before. As a result I became interested in social work and saw probably much more than I would have seen as a nurse.

I was born on Hester Street which was recently the subject of a movie on Jewish immigration. Although all Italian at that time, I remember very clearly the firehouse, which is still there, where my brother and I used to play. Many of the Italians who lived on Hester Street were from the Foggia region and, later, Neapolitans and Sicilians moved there. I do not recall any problems among the groups. We never really talked about integration of different dialect groups among ourselves, considering us all to be Italians. We moved from Manhattan to Brooklyn when I was four years old and there we joined the Baptist Church in the Williamsburg section, near the Williamsburg Bridge. There were other nationalities in the neighborhood such as Jews and Germans with whom we never had any difficulty nor with the colored people whom we met in school. We were members of the Italian Baptist Church which is still there. For years this church was on Jackson Street. When the highway was constructed, however, the church was moved to Devoe Street where it presently stands. Although there are presently more colored than white members, it is still known as the Italian Baptist Church.

Some but not all of the pastors there were Italian, but those who were not still had to get along with the Italians. I realize that, being a Protestant I come from quite a different background from most Italians. Indeed, some years ago when I was about to be given a citation by the Italian government for service to Italian immigrants, I even told the vice-consul that I was not Catholic, and he informed me that the Italian government was more interested in what I had done for the Italians than in what religion I was.

I went first to Public School 143 in Brooklyn and then to Eastern District High School but I did not graduate even though I reached my senior year. Later I took courses at Temple University when I started working in Philadelphia. Prior to Philadelphia I held a job in New York but I became tired of doing the same thing over and over again. Then, I heard about this job with the Society for the Protection of Children in Philadelphia. I knew no one there but I decided to take a chance. I got along very well with my coworkers even though I was the only Italian among the social workers. I was the first of my nationality or of any foreign background that they had ever hired in that organization. Later, they hired refugees of various backgrounds. I remember those who came from Germany who spoke in their horrible German accents could never seem to make out my name. They would go over it again and again. "What is your name?" I would answer "Carlozzi, C−A−R−L−O−Z−Z−I and it's Italian". I never forgot to tell them that it was Italian. I still got along very well with them and we cooperated with one another. For example, if they came across some Italians in the areas in which they worked they would notify me. Although I worked with other ethnic groups I specialized in problems among the Italians and also acted as an interpretor for them. In the beginning I made many house calls and had to climb many flights of stairs, which was tiring. After a while I had my clients come down to meet me.

Part of the work we did as social workers was to try to get the children of these families involved with their religion. As such, I had some difficulties with some of the Catholics who thought I was encouraging them to look upon the Protestant Church as more tolerable. My reaction was that the Catholic Church was not extending itself to look into the home conditions of the immigrants. The immigrants we met were usually surprised to find an Italian as a social worker. I understood some Italian because it was spoken by my parents at home. I learned most of my real Italian, however, from my church since we had Italian services. When I worked with the aliens on Ellis Island I did not work exclusively with Italians and was able to assist people of many nationalities. I seemed to be able to catch the intonations and the gist of what these non-English speaking immigrants wanted to say, using my hands and facial expressions to tell them what I was trying to say. They always understood me and we never had any trouble. I worked for the Society for the Protection of Children in Philadelphia from 1923 until 1934.

After my tenure in Philadelphia I decided to relocate in New York to be close to my husband. At that time Edward Corsi was the head of the Department of Welfare and although I did not know him then, I eventually came to know him and his wife quite well. He was a humane individual who was, however, not a good politician. Mrs. Corsi later became a member of the board of directors of the Italian Welfare League. Ironically, in all the years she worked among the Italians she never learned even to say "yes" in Italian. In any event I asked somebody if they could speak to Mr. Corsi on my behalf but, as it turned out, this person knew of an opportunity with the Italian Welfare League which was in need of an executive director. When I handed my resume to the League, they immediately hired me. Meanwhile the social agency in Philadelphia assured me that I could have a job with them if things did not work out in New York. I thought to myself, however, that I had never been out of work since I first started to work and I was going to succeed.

My work with the Italian Welfare League which commenced in 1934, compelled me to adapt quickly. Up to then I had never seen either a first citizenship paper or a second citizenship paper. Now, I was required to become an expert about these papers, how they were filled out, and how the questions had to be answered. I was required to speak to prospective citizens in a way which would not jeopardize their confidence in me. That, however, was not the end of the procedure. There was so much important paper work involved that if I did not take their cases without previously clearing up the complications involved, they would have been deported. I had to fight for them. I was not going against the United States, but I was looking out for the interests of these immigrants.

The Italian Welfare League was organized after World War I by the Italian Division of the American Red Cross. The initiators included Mrs. Corerra, a fine person and an Italian Jewess, Miss DeReti, an Italian American daughter of a well known New York doctor, and Mrs. DiGiorgio among others. We had to survive strictly by contributions. We never charged people for our services although some wanted to make contributions anyway, which made it possible for us to continue. We always instructed aliens who wanted to contribute to make their checks out to the League not to the individuals who took on their case. Indeed, we had to get rid of a couple of people who took money directly. One time, I remember, I was criticized for working with the Jews. I said that I worked with the Jews when they had trouble with Mussolini since they had called me in and asked me to help them. These were refugees from Mussolini and, although Jews, were nevertheless from Italy.

Much of my work in the early years of the League was involved with assisting Italian immigrants who had incurred the official displeasure of the Immigration Office. These were the post-1924 years in which all the new immigrants had to be in possession of a document showing they had come in legally. Unaware that it was still possible to enter the country legally, these people resorted to illegal entry and then found it necessary to legitimatize their status or face deportation regardless of whether they had wives and children. The head of the Immigration Office at Ellis Island asked us if we would do something about these people, to help them straighten out their status prior to deportation. The authorities were anxious to have the situation corrected because they did not know what to do with the families that would be left after the husbands were deported. Thus, we now started working with the wives and children who, in many instances, were *bona fide* United States citizens and could not be deported with the illegal aliens. We tried to help in whatever way we could by filling out the necessary forms and by obtaining correct documents and the like for approval by the Immigration Office. If these prospective deportees could not be helped the frequent result was broken families. These were the years of the depression and, without the breadwinner at home, it was very difficult for the rest of the family. The wives often could not get work so we tried to assist. Since we were bilingual it was easy for us to help out families who did not speak English and complete the necessary forms for assistance.

In addition to legal help we also tried to get jobs for the wives. We tried to help those who could not work to get relief by explaining their plight to the relief officials. We worked very hard in those days because the immigrants were, for the most part, ignorant of the laws involved. Sometimes, the results were humorous. I remember one day a woman came to me and said "I need four tires for my car", I said, "I wish I had a car". She thought I was being facetious since she really did not know that the relief was for food and not for luxuries. Many times we were presented with problems for which we did not have a ready reply. We would then have to scout around to see what the answers were.

To get to Ellis Island you had to go by a ferry which came only once every hour. On my very first day I missed the boat. There were other people on Ellis Island who had been incarcerated there and needed clothing, shaving material, toothpaste and other little necessities of this sort. The money to pay for these supplies came largely from our organization while the food was supplied by the government. Until the immigrants became accustomed to this food more was thrown out than was eaten.

I was not so horribly impressed when I first went to work on the Island because I had previously worked in a settlement house with similar types of people. In addition, I was anxious to help the Italians incarcerated there. My anxiety increased, however, when I learned that many of them being held there were victims of an overzealous official who had accidently misled them into giving wrong answers, or who was too punctilious about rules. During the war we had thousands of people on the Island. After December 7, 1941 the FBI rounded up Italians, Germans and Japanese and brought them to Ellis Island where they slept in great dorms with double beds. For the most part, they were separated according to nationality. There was an interesting case of an immigrant who swept the dorm. He had lost his alien registration card and had come to the Island to report it six months earlier. Upon informing the authorities, he was told to wait until they could get around to him. Meanwhile, six months had passed. I went to the head of the Immigration Service and asked him if he ever checked his cases and I proceeded to tell him about the sweeper. The sweeper was then released and I put him into contact with his relatives who met him in Manhattan. Ironically, he had proved his loyalty to his adopted land by picking up empty cigarette packs and taking out the lead wrappings used then, and packing them into a sizeable ball. When I asked him what he was doing it he said, "I am working for the war effort". I went back to the immigration inspector and told him that if they had a better American on the Island they would have to show him to us.

We had many similar cases. My most memorable one is a story about this girl whose mother, a United States citizen living in Italy, had sent her daughter to the United States to live with relatives. These relatives, who lived in Binghamton, New York, did not want her and notified us of their decision. As it happened, she had a paraplegic cousin who agreed to take her, assuring me that he and his wife did want her and could take care of her. He told me to call the Bulova Watch Company for his reference. I told the girl she could live with her cousin, but that if she returned to Italy she could not stay there for more than a year. Eventually, she went back to Italy for a visit and I arranged for her to have a good place on the ship with good people. Less than a year afterward, I heard through the grapevine that she was back. Seeking her out I found that she had married a cousin in Italy whom she could call into the United States. Some months later she informed me that she had been a second prize winner on the Irish Sweepstakes, winning $56,000, of which she never sent one cent to the League. I was disappointed in this because we had done so much for her. Without us she would have been left stranded on the street.

At the end of World War II there were a number of Italian war brides who came to Ellis Island and the Italian Welfare League interpreted for them and informed them of the requirements for lawful admission to the United States. For example, they would have to have $500 to assure the American government that, in case the young man refused to marry the Italian girl, she would have enough fare to return to Italy. A number of human interest stories emerged from this experience: some happy, some sad and some humane. I remember one little young lady who came to meet her boyfriend to get married, only to find out that he had married someone else. In the meantime, the boy's uncle came to see the girl every two weeks while she was waiting for the necessary paper work to return to Italy. Well, one day I was on a ship which had just arrived and was assisting in the interpreting, when I heard "Signora, Signora", and sure enough this girl, Marta, ran to me and told me that she had married the uncle and was now entering on a visa as the wife of an American citizen.

I also remember meeting one Italian girl on Ellis Island who was crying because her boyfriend had not come to meet her. All was not lost, however, because she had met a Japanese man and was going to marry him. She had been kept on the Island for some time during which she attempted suicide merely because she wanted to get off the Island. I told her she should not attempt that again because she would be sent back to Italy thereby extracting a promise that she would behave. In the meantime her Japanese boyfriend came with plenty of money to cover her bond. She married him and went to live with him in Hawaii.

On Ellis Island there were many service groups like the Italian Welfare League. We shared one big room, where each of the nationalities had a desk. The British and the Irish fought all the time. I really enjoyed my work even though it was very hard. Sometimes, my feet would be swollen because of all the walking I would do on the piers and I would go home, soak them, and be anxious to return the next morning.

Ellis Island was close to the Jersey shore, a region which was narrow, but very treacherous. The water ran by very swiftly. I remember one girl who came up to me once and said "Why don't you just give me a yellow paper so then I can get out of the hospital". I was unable to give her the paper, and she said that she was going to swim. I responded: "we will find you in the water in a couple of days". Later, that was precisely what happened. I kept warning people against trying to swim the treacherous water. There were signs and gates placed in the path, but to some it seemed so inviting because the distance seemed so small. I do not remember many who really tried to or who actually committed suicide. Incidentally, the consul also warned them against trying to swim the distance since his office had to pay for the burial.

For the most part there were no unique problems for Italians on Ellis Island. Basically they were kind of slow and docile and they would entertain themselves by playing mandolins, guitars, etc. The Germans, on the other hand, were very aggressive.

Our League did a lot of work but we did not take care of all the Italians who entered Ellis Island. It would have been impossible to do so since ours was a small operation. We tended to handle special cases which the immigration officials referred to us or those who sought us out.

We had an unemployment service where we searched out Italian employers and referred our cases to them. Most of these employed artisans and manual laborers. We did not have to do anything in the construction trade since most of them had relatives, or *paesani* to get them into the trade. Even today many Italian immigrants are in construction. I also worked with an assistant of the unionist, Luigi Antonini, to place workers in the garment trade.

When World War II came, all the Italian sailors from the Italian ships in American ports were also shipped to Ellis Island. It was Roosevelt's idea to gather these sailors, even to the extent of going to South American countries and taking Italian sailors from Italian ships docked there, and bring them to the United States. He claimed they had to be interned because they were sabotaging ships. This was not so at all. I was very outspoken about this and probably jeopardized myself. In fact, my husband wondered aloud how I was never arrested. I rebuked American officials at Ellis Island in behalf of these Italian sailors saying that whatever they did to American ships was done in response to orders. They were, after all, Italians. There were hundreds of them on Ellis Island sleeping in double beds in a large room on the Island. Interned there were also a great many German people even women who had been placed there by the FBI. The FBI was very vigilant at that time. The Japanese were of course put into internment camps which I thought was bad because they were American citizens and not Japanese. I did not hesitate to tell the authorities that we were doing something wrong in this regard. The Italian sailors held on Ellis Island were not American citizens. Interestingly, a few of them were sent to Texas, where state authorities did not know what to do with them. Texas had no internment camps so they were kept in prisons until 10:00 at night when they were let out and allowed to cook for everybody there.

Our organization was also involved when Italians were required to register in the post office as aliens. I was one of the leaders who organized a group and pressured the New York Post Office to allow our representatives to assist Italian immigrants in filling out official papers, etc. The Immigration Office rules were such that a minor error could cause a great deal of trouble. We found one man who had come here in 1885 and had moved once. When he first came he lived at 136 Mott Street, let us say, and then moved to 164 Mott Street. That constituted the only move he had made in the United States yet he was called in by the authorities on the grounds that his residency in the country was in question. Someone had to speak in behalf of these people or they could be accused of being enemy aliens. There was another man who had lost his arm during World War I who told the FBI where the Americans could drop their bombs over Italy since he knew the country. I reproached him saying, "Aren't you ashamed of yourself telling these people where they should drop bombs. Let them find out for themselves. This is war and you are not in it. You are only an internee." He looked at me startled and I said "Yes, look at me. If it were up to me you would be in jail."

A number of internees were released after investigation proved there were no grounds on which to hold them. I remember one time when I was instrumental in gaining the release of a large number of men who were to be released in their own recognizance after they posted $500 bonds. I informed them that they would not have to put up the money since they would be released anyway. This was part of my work as the official representative of the Italian Welfare League on Ellis Island. It was my responsibility to look after the legitimate interest of the Italian immigrants and aliens and I was conversant with the whole operation on Ellis Island. I also used to go to Washington once a month on cases to appear before the

Board of Immigration Appeals. I had my license to practice before the Board in 1944. The Board members would listen carefully to my arguments on each case and then would tell me that they would inform me of their decision. Only one of my cases was deported in all of the 18 years I was there and this person was deported largely because I did not know the ropes when I first began. After that, however, I became much more familiar with the practices and legal traps. My work was a tremendous sense of satisfaction to me. If I had the strength I would go back to it today. Of course, it is entirely different today than it was in those years, but I would go back because it was a source of wonderful satisfaction to me. I was sometimes sworn at and, many things were said about me, but a simple "Thank you", wiped out everything else.

We had an office on Ellis Island and in New York City. There was a counterpart of our organization in California but they did not work as we did. Each of the groups worked differently. There were other societies which should have helped but one wonders what they did. For example, when a group in Queens was complaining of too many Italian immigrants requesting its help in gaining naturalization I offered to assist their office, but they did not take the offer. Similarly we never worked with any other Italian organization. Other groups working along the same lines have been initiated more recently, like ACIM (American Committee on Italian Migration) but they are latecomers. I was the only full-time employee for the Italian Welfare League at that time. Eventually I finally retired and shortly afterwards the League closed its office. I only regretted that I had not trained anyone to take over when I retired.

Some Italian American leaders like Vito Marcantonio did help us. One event in which he was particularly interested concerned Dominick Trombetta, a family friend and a notorious pro-fascist before the war. Trombetta had openly espoused Mussolini and published a facist Italian American newspaper. At one point, however, Trombetta made the mistake of falsely claiming American citizenship, which caused the immigration authorities to pick him up and intern him on Ellis Island as an unfriendly alien. For him to gain release it would require approval of the Ellis Island Appeals Board whose membership included Luigi Antonini, the labor leader and opponent of Trombetta. It seems they had a feud going back many years when someone was killed on Staten Island at a rally. Trombetta informed me that Antonini would never agreed to his release. "You know Angela", he said to me, "I just heard Antonini say that I would never get off the Island unless I came down to him on my knees begging forgiveness about the Staten Island affair". I was angry and called Marcantonio identifying myself as a social worker from Ellis Island, telling him it was important that I come to speak with him. He consented and I went to see him that very afternoon, aware, of course of the differences between Marcantonio and Antonini. After I told Marcantonio what I had heard about Antonini's threat against Trombetta, Marcantonio responded that he would have the man off the Island that afternoon, which was exactly what happened. When I returned to Ellis Island to tell Trombetta what Marcantonio had promised I was very happy because I felt sorry for Trombetta. Even though he spoke pro-fascist before the war, after the war broke out he closed down his paper and said that now we were all required to work for America. He was a pitiable man. When it came time for his hearing on Ellis Island, with the exception of my husband, none of his former friends came out to testify in his behalf. Trombetta was very happy when he was released. You never saw a man cry the way he did over his joy at leaving the Island. You must remember he was treated as a prisoner and that when they took him to Washington he was held with manacles on his hands and feet.

I remember one time when I had to plead before Department of Justice officials in behalf of two northern Italian immigrants Marie and Mario Borrino who were husband and wife. We had become quite friendly and I advised them to become citizens and prepare for certain questions when they appeared before the Board in Washington. Despite my preparations, however, they said something wrong and were turned down in their citizenship request. Six months had to elapse before they could apply again. I told them that I would go down in their stead when the time came, which I did. Facing a board of seven or eight rat-faced men if ever I saw one, you would think I was on trial. Initially, of course, they inquired whether I was a fascist. I replied, "No, unless attendance at American public schools made me a fascist". I remember one of them noticed that I lived in Greenwich Village and asked me about the Italian boys in the village. I said, "Stop right there, they are not Italian boys, they are Americans and they are doing their job for this, their native country". I also reminded them that boys from the Village were in the army and fighting for the United States. The Board was obviously baiting me to show the two people I was representing in the worst possible way. Where I could make a point, however, I never gave them a yes or no answer preferring long answers instead. These Board of Immigration Appeal sessions were put on tape and kept confidential.

Antonini had his own workers with whom we worked on occasion but he did not have that much expertise in these matters. He did, however, have many contacts which we found useful. The unions had a great deal of money but they never gave us any. We deliberately had nothing to do with the politicians because we would do all the work and they would take all the credit. We did work with the priests and church groups within specific denominations.

I remember the time that the ship *Gripsholm* was sent back to Italy filled with Italian seamen who had been interned here. One of these seamen came to me with tears in his eyes because his name had been taken off the list and he was not going to return. He asked that I please put him on the list for returnees since it was seven years since he had seen his family. I was able to help him. I remember also that there was a huge pile of clothing that these Italian seamen had bought with their own money. This clothing was put into the yard at Ellis Island because some dopey coastguardsman said that Italian officials would not permit it to enter Italy. I got on the phone quickly and called the Italian consulate, which was staffed by some lower echelon officials, and I asked one of them to get in touch with the State Department and tell them that the Italian seamen's clothing was being taken away because of a report that the Italian government would not permit it to enter. He cleared it up that afternoon.

Near the end of my career with the Italian Welfare League, I became disappointed with some of the new people on the board who did not seem to appreciate the service and type of work we were performing. They were too concerned with the monetary expenditures.

Today there are more Italian Americans involved in social work than ever before but they do not speak Italian. I even inaugurated a scholarship at the Columbia School of Social Work for an Italian man or woman, who would use Italian after they graduated in their work, but it was never taken.

The immigrants coming from Italy today, I would say, are better educated, a factor most noticeable within the last several years. I always encouraged Italian immigrants, even the sweepers at Ellis Island, to go to school. A number of them did and they became agents at the facility. Newcomers today, also dress better than the earlier comers. I know that the people who came right after World War II were generally poorly dressed and not well-educated. Many of them even still make their own clothes.

Frank J Tarallo

I was born on October 29, 1913, in Middletown, Connecticut, in what was then called "Little Italy", a section close to the Connecticut River. I was born on the second floor of a spaghetti processing plant owned by the Zantis who were very generous people and especially helpful to newly-arrived immigrants. From there my family moved to Ferry Street which is another section of Little Italy. The boundaries of Middletown's Little Italy in the pre-World War I and postwar period included Ferry Street, College Street, William Street, Court Street, Center Street, which no longer exists, and Rapallo Avenue. It extends north as far as St. John's Street, to St. John's Church.

My childhood recollections are mostly of close family ties and an almost daily arrival of immigrants, friends and cousins. I clearly remember when I was about eight or nine years old, going to meet the Middletown and Hartford boats, which brought the immigrants to the Connecticut area from Ellis Island. We waited at the dock and I remember all sorts of shouting, greetings and singing to relatives who had arrived. I remember the immigrants had to climb the dirt path across the railroad tracks to the customs house where officials checked the baggages and bundles which consisted mainly of salami, cheese and onions. Each was permitted through once he had left a slice of salami, a piece of cheese or onions. The customs house had the lists of those coming from Italy so relatives here were able to find out when these people were due in from New York.

The route for most of the immigrants who came to Connecticut was generally up the Connecticut River from Ellis Island to Hartford. Virtually all the immigrants from Melilli, Sicily, however, settled in Middletown. At the customs house sometimes there would be some individuals from other groups looking out for the people coming from Melilli because their relatives might not be able to get off from work to meet them. The customs office there had been at the same location since Connecticut was still an English colony. Ships then came from England and proceeded directly up the Connecticut River. For years the customs office had been closed, until the immigrants started coming.

My mother was 13 when she came to the United States and my father was 15. My father passed away when he was 69 and my mother is still living at 82. My parents were part of a continual flow of citizens from "Meliddi" or Melilli as they say in Italian, to Middletown. My mother, like many other immigrants was *hospide*. That is, she was brought to the United States with a "guarantee letter" that her two (twin) older sisters who had preceeded her here would take care of her. My father was "guaranteed" by a friend of the family. They, in turn, did the same for my grandmother a few years afterward.

When my father first arrived, he worked as most of his *paesani* emigrés did, in a *shoppe di carzalore,* or tin shop where they made pots and pans. Many also worked in the Russell Manufacturing Company, which had two or three plants and was the largest employer in the town. The immigrants engaged in a kind of skilled work, running weaving machines from which the company manufactured suspenders. My aunts made button holes in the suspenders, a type of work engaged in by many Italian women. Because of the better salaries, stronger Italian immigrants applied for work at the Pintchock factory where they made utensils for kitchens.

The Mellillesi were religious and Catholic and went to St. John's School because it was the only one which taught religion. St. John's was not our parish and was on the other side of town, but we all still attended church there. Because it was not our parish, there was a little irritation reflected when the immigrants were reluctant to take seats in the front of the church. We were embarrassed and a bit ashamed since the services were exclusively in English which we could not understand. Not much was done by the church to cater to the needs of these immigrants. This was probably because the migration was a massive one and too abrupt for the church to make quick adjustments. At the same time they welcomed us and were very warm and receptive. I remember all the nuns as wonderful and very understanding of our language barrier. It was at St. John's that I was baptized, learned English, became an altar boy, a choir boy and was trained into the Christian religion and church affairs.

From St. John's I attended Middletown High School from 1928 to 1932. The teaching at St. John's had given us a good foundation in English thereby facilitating acculturation and assimilation. In high school through participation in athletics, debating clubs and the like I began to establish friendships with Protestants and others with whom I formerly had no contact. Most of the football players were Irish and Italian, and many went on to college such as Nick Cubetta, now a retired dentist, who went to Catholic University.

Having played four years of high school football, I was given a try-out scholarship at the University of Alabama. This was called a walk-on scholarship. That is, if you proved yourself then you would be given a scholarship. Unfortunately, I injured my back and had to give up football, although I remained active in intramural sports. I finally received a B.S. in Education and Foreign Languages. My education was a strain on my family because of limited finances so I worked first in a coat factory to save my money. I also had a single aunt who helped with my expenses and at college I hopped tables at night. The University of Alabama had about 8,000 students of whom probably fewer than two hundred were Italian, although quite a few of the Italians were from Middletown.

The University then had a Reserve Officers Training Corps (ROTC) program of which I was a member. Since I graduated in the top third of my class, I received a commission in the United States Army Reserves as a second lieutenant. There was also a law which permitted some ROTC students to go to a special program from which a select few would receive regular army commissions. Unfortunately, I was not among the group selected and, after terminating my one year of active duty, I was released and I went to Hartford, Connecticut, where I worked for the Hartford *Retreat* newspaper. I had planned to go to Chicago, but it was 1939 and the army had started to recall a number of men of whom I was one. Initially, I went into the First Infantry division but later I was transferred to the amphibious training center. I remember when I went home to Connecticut that Christmas my sister called saying there was a telegram for me from the War Department ordering me to report to Washington, D.C. That was my entry into OSS.

I did not know what OSS was all about at the time, but I soon found out through Max Corvo a good friend of mine from Middletown. He was then the director of Special Intelligence. He had become involved through Earl Brennan, who was chosen by OSS director, William Donovan to create the Special Intelligence (S.I.) section. Brennan recruited Max Corvo as the first member of his staff (the S.I. staff). Max, in turn recruited about a dozen Sicilian Americans most of whom were from the close knit Italian communities of Middletown, and Hartford, to form the nucleus of Brennan's operation. S.I. (Special Intelligence) was designed to gather information rather than enter combat. When Max Corvo had first enlisted in the army, he had an idea, a dream, in which he persisted while carrying on his menial tasks as an army private. He possessed a rich background of experience gleaned from his father who was an anti-fascist leader who had been forced to leave Italy when Mussolini came to power. Cesare Corvo, Max's father was well versed in the history of Italy, and he communicated this interest to his son. Max realized at the time of his appointment to S.I. that it was important to have people in proper positions who were familiar with Sicily. He had the temerity to approach Russell, for whom he had worked as a youngster in Middletown, with the object of having himself recognized as an authority on intelligence regarding Sicily, emphasizing the desirability of assembling individuals with experience to be assigned to OSS. Russell contacted Middletown resident Dean Acheson who later became Secretary of State. Acheson, of course knew of the Corvos through Cesare's newspaper, *The Middletown Bulletin* (the Italian American newspaper in town), and of course he knew about Max because Max was fluent in both Italian and English and was well known in the community. Max served as correspondent for his father's paper and traveled around getting information and ads. As a result of this background Acheson brought Max Corvo into the OSS picture primarily to help the United States to establish a network of information and intelligence. His rich background in Italy and Sicily was used to assist the government in operations planned for the area.

Although I do not know for certain, I believe that it was as a result of this background that Corvo was brought to the attention of General Donovan and through Donovan to Roosevelt. Through military channels Corvo was then placed under Earl Brennan, who was chief of the S.I. in the Mediterranean, primarily Italy. Prior to the war Brennan had been in the American diplomatic corps in Italy and had become well acquainted with the Pope and with the Italian authorities.

The first person I met after I reported to Washington was Max who told me he had chosen me because of my knowledge of the Sicilian language, Sicilian life and the island itself. When we were younger we both lived on Ferry Street and we were always talking about Melilli and Sicily. Although I had never been there I was well acquainted with the mores of the people and the location of the cities. When I used to go to Mr. Corvo's *Bulletin* office there were maps of Sicily on the wall and a variety of literature available on the island. Once I arrived in Washington I learned that I was not the only one from Middletown. There was Sebastian Pasanesi, an architect who had graduated from Catholic University and was now a captain in the Marines. There was Vincent Scamparino, a lawyer who had graduated from Boston University. There was Louis Fiorilla, a Wesleyan University graduate, who became our radio operator. Then we picked up Samuel Frolino, a lawyer and graduate of Boston College, whom we met in Palermo. We also picked up four other Italian Americans from outside the Middletown area. Thus, on one mission, we were joined by "Jumping Joe Savoldi" of Notre Dame, who was recruited into OSS for a mission to pick up an Italian admiral and scientist whom the navy wanted to get out of Italy. Joe Savoldi was supposed to be a bodyguard and was assigned to assist in what proved to be a successful operation. Admiral Minicini was a reserve officer in the Italian Navy who could be equated with our Admiral Rickover. Minicini was held under a type of house arrest with his wife and required to carry on scientific experiments for the Italian navy near Naples. There was also an OSS operation carried out in which he and his wife were put on a boat and taken out of Italy. I had been on the island of Ventetene and then on Capri when I was instructed to accompany the admiral and his wife to Palermo. The whole mission was initiated by Max Corvo and approved by American naval officers. Corvo debriefed Minicini and gained valuable information. The navy then flew the admiral to the United States where he was placed in a research lab on Rhode Island.

My S.I. group reported to Casablanca in October 1942 and from there it went to Algiers where the AFH (Allied Forces Headquarters) under General Eisenhower was stationed. At this time the Allied command was planning the invasion of Sicily. The detailed information possessed by Max Corvo about the island was transmitted to Brennan, and to Scamporini, who was liaison with allied forces in Algiers, and finally to G-2 which used it according to strategy. Corvo's S.I. group went to Sicily in July 1943 and was used to obtain combat information as requested by the S-2 sections of the various regiments under General Patton. We infiltrated our agents through and behind enemy lines where they posed as native Italians. Our commanding officer who accompanied us was Col. William A. Eddy, a Marine who had participated in World War I and who spoke many languages fluently. I was then stationed at General Patton's G-2 headquarters as a representative. Whenever Patton needed information behind the lines his intelligence officer, G-2 Colonel Carter gave the directions which I related to

Max Corvo who then gave me the infiltration team that I needed to approach the front lines with the representative of the S-2 which was regimental intelligence. They would ask us whether we could perform a certain mission. I would study the situation, prepare the team and under the cover of darkness and dressed in civilian clothes traveled to the front lines in a jeep. As it turned out we were rather successful obtaining the necessary information about German concentrations, tanks and ammunition dumps. This information covered territory from the southern part of Sicily to Palermo.

From the moment we landed in Sicily, Corvo was busy recruiting local agents to reinforce our groups. The natives proved cooperative, helpful and willing. They came from various walks of life; from the Italian armed forces, from political backgrounds, from prisoners of war we had freed, etc.

In a way it was a somewhat traumatic experience among Italian Americans fighting in Italy, but it was isolated because I knew that our relatives were in Melilli. We had landed in Licara which was in the central part of Sicily so actually we were not directly concerned with our area. It was a difficult experience in a way since we knew that our villages were being bombed and that there was a war going on, on all parts of the island. I knew I had cousins in Sicily about my age whom I had never seen and I was concerned about that. Whenever we did find prisoners I was looking for names among them to see if any were my relatives and then hoped to recruit them.

During a brief period of rest, Max Corvo gave me permission to visit Melilli because he knew I had wanted to visit my relatives there. I went with another friend in a jeep loaded with what were then "goodies" (cigarettes, coffee, sugar) — items which we were authorized by the military government to dispense with as a means of spreading as much good will as possible among the natives. With that in mind we went to Melilli and, as I was going up the dirt road in the jeep, I realized that we must have presented quite a sight — dirty, with two weeks growth of beard and worn-out clothes. As I approached the plaza I saw this little old man sitting there. I stopped the jeep and was about to ask him directions when all of a sudden he jumped up and said, *"Figlio mio, figlio mio"*. It was my grandfather holding my high school picture in his lap. From there we went to see Louis Fiorillo's uncle who was a priest at the mother church which they call *la matrice*. We stayed there and met all the rest of the relatives. In the meantime, I was surveying my relatives to discern whether any of them could be helpful with any kind of military intelligence. They were all definitely country people and none of them had the kind of qualifications we needed. Thus, the visit remained a family thing without military significance.

During the two and a half years I was involved in SI/OSS, I never killed anyone and I never fired a shot. This phenomenon was a living affirmation of the concept of our section to gather information and disappear, "Don't fight, don't shoot, don't kill". OSS instruction in formalized schools was very thorough, and taught us the various ways of gathering intelligence and bringing it back at all costs without engaging in any kind of hostile activities. I do not know of any case in which any of the natives were killed because of our endeavor to achieve our mission. The natives were cooperative as were our relatives. The question of fascism or anti-fascism or socialism or any other ideology did not arise because they were all so enthusiastic to see the American troops. The Italian army did not present a great obstacle either. The Italian forces in Sicily at the time were absolutely down in spirits, and they did not want to fight. They had had a traumatic experience in North Africa where they were badly defeated by the American and British forces. They were cooperative and helpful. We used them in the mess halls, officers clubs and motor pools. They were quite happy when the Americans came. As a matter of fact, until the Allied lines overran their areas many of these troops had been hiding in caves by the thousands.

With respect to the mafia-type element in the SI or OSS, as far as I recall there never was any incident or any indication that the mafia was associated with SI missions or operations in Sicily or Italy. I say that with conviction and emphasis even though some contend to the contrary. I am currently reading Harris R. Smith, *OSS A Secret History of America's First Central Intelligence Agency,* who contends that Washington officials complained about mafia-type packs working in Glavin's command. Glavin was one of our commanding officers in Italy and he is quoted as saying that many Italian "hoods" were recruited by the OSS. That is plain hogwash. In the same book, on another page, Smith mentions that Corvo recruited his people largely from Middletown or from other parts such as Long Island, Brooklyn, Michigan or California, but none of these people were criminals. One of them was a police officer. Another was a son of Visceglia, the wine grower in California and a football player at the University of Alabama. These were the types recruited into the SI.

Among the main assignments, those of substantial priority included liberating political prisoners interned on the Mediterranean Islands. We were in possession of reports indicating that among the prisoners in the Italian archipelago were political prisoners incarcerated by the Mussolini regime over the preceding ten or fifteen years. Many of them were rather important individuals, such as government figures, political figures and the intelligentsia who could not go along with fascism. One of our primary targets was the island of Ventetene because it coincided with the landing of General Mark Clark's forces at Salerno. After the landing there, Admiral King convened a conference aboard the battleship off the Bay of Palermo. The S.I./OSS was represented at the conference through the participation of Max Corvo and Vincent Scamparino. It was determined that we were to act as a diversionary task force (80.4 task force). Our group consisted of a nucleus of S.I. Italian OSS personnel under my command, and was joined by six other members of the OSS all trained for this type of activity. Ventetene Island is known as the "Island of Ill Wind" and is located about 18 miles due northwest from the Bay of Naples (southwest of it is the Island of Capri, south of it is the Island of Ischia and southwest was the Salerno landing). Our leaving the port of Palermo and heading due north was used as a diversion from Clark's armada causing German espionage to think that we were the expected landing force. We crossed Mark Clark's convoy which left North Africa and was going from west to east outside the Bay of Palermo. That was a marvelous idea because it led the Germans to believe that they were going to the Balkans or the Adriatic. In the role of a decoy we proceeded to approach the island which intelligence reports had led us to believe was occupied only by political prisoners without any German personnel (on a nearby island there were also about 5,000 political prisoners which we liberated).

Because of the frequent bombardment over a number of years the Ventetene natives had abandoned their homes and lived in caves. I remember one young priest on the island living with the people in caves and caring for them as best he could. Bedsheets marked the individual apartments in which they all slept and ate. After we cleaned out the apartments and the homes and defumigated them we finally moved the people out of the caves. Then the military government came in and helped them with food, medicine and other things.

We got to the island by boat, on the destroyer *USS Knight* which was part of a fleet of vessels.

Much to our surprise and contrary to the intelligence that we had received prior to leaving Palermo, we found out that on the main Ventetene Island there were Germans, 89 in all. We were told that the objective was to establish a radar screen for our air force stationed in Sardinia. Then we were to offer umbrella cover for our aircraft which was flying out of

Brindisi up the Adriatic on what was called the "milk run". This was the one which bombarded the Ploesti oil fields. Our mission, then, was threefold: 1) to deceive the Germans about the Salerno landings; 2) to recoup all the political prisoners in the area; and 3) to set up a beacon for our radar so that our fighter planes from Sardinia would pick up our bombers in the vicinity of Verona. A lieutenant from A-2, which was Air Force intelligence was supposed to set up this beacon. Since, however, we were attracting small arms fire from the port, we found out that this beacon was not going to be easy. Faced with this unexpected obstacle, Alberto Braccho, an architect who had been a prisoner of the fascists for 18 years, was an anti-fascist from a notable family in Palermo. Braccho helped us negotiate surrender terms with the Ventetene Island Germans, which we finally did after a harrowing experience. The experience was later written into a popular story entitled *A Ragged Crew,* by John Steinbeck. Unfortunately, Steinbeck did not give credit to S.I. personnel, nor to the original crew I headed. He gave credit to a parachute lieutenant who never existed.

In effecting the surrender of the Germans at Ventetene Island, the surprising thing was that although there was a minimum of firing, there were no casualties on either side. Alberto Braccho proposed going up to the Germans with a white flag and talking to the lieutenant telling him that a destroyer was coming in behind us. Evidently he succeeded in convincing the German Lieutenant Eingler because when he came down the path from the hill he said, "Look, they want to negotiate. I want you two men to walk halfway up the path, while I go back to the German and bring him halfway down to meet." Braccho came back with the Germans and we negotiated and they believed me when I told them that if they did not surrender unconditionally, the island would be blown off the face of the map. The German lieutenant saw the destroyer, which, by the way was actually going toward Salerno and had no intention at all of protecting us. We were so convincing with Braccho speaking fluent Italian and fluent German, we engineered the entire thing. When the German lieutenant became convinced of the impossibility of his situation he conversed with the other two German lieutenants who also were convinced to surrender. They surrendered their arms and we were joined by Captain Holland who had his men stand guard as the line of German soldiers came down the mountainside. We put them in the *caserma* (jail) and signed the armistice terms of which I still have a copy. This mission took place on September 8, 1943 and because of it I was awarded a cluster to a previously won silver star. The mission was entirely successful in its three-fold objective; we did deceive the Germans; we liberated many prisoners in the Ventetene archipelago; and we liberated the islands making it possible to erect a radar beacon. The first silver star I won was for the liberation of the Lipari Island group which was made famous by the movie *The Stromboli.*

The complete report on the mission was radioed to Palermo and from there relayed to Eisenhower's Allied General headquarters in North Africa in Algiers. In the reports I transmitted all the information I had gleaned from the operation including intelligence news about fortifications, etc. At the same time, I was also recommended for a Navy Cross by Captain Andrews, commander of the *USS Knight.*

The Lipari archipelago of which Lipari was the largest island, was located off the northern coast of Sicily. The mission complement consisted of myself, Pvt. North, Pvt. Fiorilla, Pvt. Treglia, Pvt. Durante, Pvt. Clemente, Pvt. Bellardo, who owns a restaurant in New York, Carl Bonmarito and Pvt. Cambiolo. It also included a Navy lieutenant, who was a graduate of Wesleyan and who commanded three P.T. boats. The purpose of the Lipari mission was to retrieve Italian personnel whom we knew we could use either as agents or as personnel within the OSS operations.

In possession of some information about the prisoners on the island we thought it wiser to utilize Italian American personnel in these undertakings since it was expected that they would more readily be accepted by the Italians. Thus, to the natives it was not as if they were surrendering, but was more of a liberation since they had been suffering for so long from the fascist regime. The act of freeing them, in addition to the fact that we spoke the language, the dialect, and had names like theirs, made it much easier for us to gather valuable information such as the names of the leaders in the various cities and in Palermo, and a list of people aggravating the situation against the Americans. Sometimes we even had the advantage of blood relationship, which was usually discovered through the general process of interrogation. Thus, some uncovered the fact that they had a common great grandfather or a common uncle. We accumulated this information, briefed the political prisoners and turned them over to G-3 to General Patton and the Seventh Army. Aside from gathering this information and turning it over to the proper headquarters, we were also able to establish bases throughout the Mediterranean area. This was very valuable since the Americans and the British used the bases to harass German sealanes and supply lines from Genoa, to La Spezia and Salerno and other places in the area. This was, incidentally, another reason the PT squadrons accompanied us on these missions, since they could then use the bases for refueling and for night observation of Axis traffic in the Mediterranean.

Since the Lipari Islands are off the northeast coast of Sicily, between the mainland and Sicily they are strategically located to observe and intercept all kinds of traffic coming from the Ionian Sea or going into the Mediterranean, North Africa, etc. The Islands housed approximately 8,000 natives and prisoners. Of the latter the majority were political prisoners who could not accept the fascist regime in Italy, or who posed a threat to Mussolini either through jealousy, or through differences of opinion, not necessarily political.

There were no women in these prison camps. For some reason in Italy during the war women did not seem to play a major role since they did not pose a major threat to the regime and thus there seemed to be little need to imprison many of them. The fascists knew that the women were clever and that they did play a part, if not openly. When I was on the Island of Prochida, which is near Naples, a young woman whose father was a postman in Naples was of great assistance to me. She was always sending me valuable information by rowing back and forth with the mail to the island from Naples. She was anti-fascist and was one of many Italian women who worked with us as agents, couriers, etc.

There were not many Italian priests who were political prisoners. The Italian government generally was tolerant of the clergy because they knew that the priests were helping people with food and clothing but not politically. None of them that we knew, in the two and a half years I was in Italy, were jailed. The fascists adopted a *laissez faire* attitude toward the priests.

On the Lipari mission we did not encounter German personnel resistance. Rather, the island had a small contingent of Italian naval personnel. One of them, a lieutenant, surrendered his sword when we arrived. On the other hand, some attempted to burn documents which we intercepted and were partly able to recuperate. These turned out to be Navy code books which proved very helpful to the United States Navy. We then reported back to Palermo and I wrote out a report which was sent to General Patton's headquarters, G-2.

We were rather lucky that the destroyer *Knight* accompanied us on this mission, because as we approached the Lipari port we noticed that on the high ridges which skirt the port were placed fully-loaded mortars. There also were machine guns and other weapons pointed at us. The presence of the destroyer *Knight*, however, neutralized their actions. When we landed we realized how fortunate we were as all these sights were zeroed in on our positions.

My family at home did not know exactly where I was although they had some idea. By tying in the contacts made by Corvo and our furloughs which coincided and brought us together, they surmised we were involved in some operation having to do with Italy, but exactly what it was they did not know. With this in mind it is interesting to note that they did not resent our actions. They thought it was wonderful that we were going to Italy, and that if we lived through it we would want to help the people. They were also resigned to the fact that we might die. Basically, however, they tended to feel that "if you were going to die, you might as well die in Italy than die in some strange place". That was also the concept we were raised with. Even though we were in the armed forces and were going to complete our mission, my father's theory was "Son, I would just as soon have you in Italy, and even if you are going to die, I can be proud of the fact that you died in my home country". In the front window of our house on Lawn Avenue, my mother had four stars displayed representing four sons in the service. My father was very proud of that.

In reviewing my wartime experience, I can say I was very proud of the role Italian Americans played in bringing an end to the fascist Italian government. Because of my Italian roots, I had empathy for the sufferings as well as for the democratic aspirations of the Italian people and I was happy to have played a part.

~SIX~

The Lawyer
and
The Entreprenuer

Introduction

The avvocato *(lawyer), the businessman and the teacher have always enjoyed positions of prestige in Italian society and among Americans of Italian descent. Thus, despite the many obstacles presented, a number of Italian Americans and their children accepted and overcame the challenges as they strove to move beyond the humble work status of their parents. Frequently, those who entered these fields relied on their ethnic backgrounds to sustain them both psychologically, and practically as their co-nationals comprised much of their clientele. In entering the professions Italians and Italian Americans demonstrated an ability to adapt themselves to the opportunities of the new country and used all the facilities at their disposal for ascending continually to higher levels. Not content to settle for the vocational choices of their parents these Italians in America fixed for themselves vocational sights which, in Italy, would have remained dormant through social stratification.*

The saga of rising expectations was truer of Italian sons than it was of Italian daughters. Thus, while it may not have been an earth shattering event for an Italian son to become a lawyer, as in the case of the auto-biography of Rosario Ingargiola, it was, nevertheless, exceptional. Even more extraordinary, however, were instances of Italian daughters who emulated their brothers and pursued careers which demonstrated the individuality and perseverance of an Elvira Adorno.*

Rosario Ingargiola, is the story of a poor Sicilian immigrant who was able to enter law and enjoy a measure of success. Although Italian Americans enter college on a par with that of the nation as a whole today, relatively few went to college and completed their higher education careers* *during the period of Ingargiola's youth. Those who did, frequently studied utilitarian vocations such as medicine, law or pharmacology. Ingargiola settled upon law, although his father taught him how to work as a barber in the event he had to fall back upon the occupation of his ancestors. Ingargiola, however, was more than a journeyman lawyer. Possessing a passion for literature and poetry, he read extensively and wrote literary criticism and poetry. Thus, for a number of years his articles and poetry appeared in various Italian American journals and newspapers. Nearing eighty, he continues to write.*

As a bright, young, Italian American lawyer he attracted considerable attention in the Italian American community of post World War I New York and became acquainted with a number of its literary and political figures including LaGuardia, Marcantonio, Schiavo, Sisca, etc. For more than a decade he was deeply involved in the fraternal activities of the Independent Order of the Sons of Italy in America. As its leading official for many years he became a participant in the life of New York City politics in general and Italian American political life in particular.

Born of immigrant parents with two of her brothers also born in Italy, Elvira Adorno, the subject of the second autobiography in this chapter, was raised in an Italian American neighborhood in New York City. At a time when to give a daughter more education than that which was required by law was considered an extravagant waste of time and money, Elvira was encouraged to extend her education. Through the support of her immigrant father she graduated New Utrecht High School in Brooklyn and went on to receive a Bachelor's Degree at Hunter College and a Master of Arts at New York University. The recipient of a Fullbright grant, Elvira Adorno taught Italian in the New York City public school system for thirty-five years. In 1963, she created the Italian Cultural Council and became its Executive Director. This Council dispenses information on all aspects of Italian language and culture. She has served the Modern Language Association in various capacities and has published a number of articles in her field.

In addition to the success story of her own career the autobiography of Elvira Adorno is included in this volume because of her accounts of the modest entrepreneurship practiced by many immigrant Italians. The story of her father's venture into the flag-making business in New York's "Little Italy" during the early part of the nineteenth century is one of the few informed accounts of this kind of activity. It demonstrates the ability of Italians to take the initiative in a land of opportunity and enter into private business while utilizing their ethnic roots to earn a living.

Rosario Ingargiola

I came to the United States in 1911 at the age of 12 with my mother while my father came later. The story of how we came to America is somewhat unusual. I had a brother who was a peculiar fellow and somewhat unruly. In fact, my father finally thought it best for him to come to America, where my father's *compare* could look after him. About 1898 or 1900 my father wrote and asked his *compare* to see if he would look after by brother and try to control him. Upon arrival in the United States my brother became a barber and wrote to us telling us of his good fortune. Years went by, then, and we never heard from him. Finally, my father again wrote to his *compare* and asked him what was happening with my brother who no longer wrote and no longer sent money. The *compare* took my brother aside and had a serious talk with him convincing him to straighten himself out and send money for the rest of the family to come, which my brother did.

My father came from the lower middle class in Italy and was a barber, although he only used the shop on Saturdays and Sundays. Monday through Friday he worked in the wineries of Marsala while my mother baked. They were very active and industrious people and although we were not rich, we managed. I also had another brother and two sisters.

I do not remember having spoken to people in Italy who had come to America previously but we did learn much from the local papers. The impression fostered by newspapers in Sicily then was that America was the "Promised Land". Indeed, America was a great opportunity for some of the immigrants from Sicily, but it was not easy. One of my uncles, for example, who came here in the 1890s went to work building tracks for the railroads throughout the country and barely made enough for a living.

My sister followed my brother here, then my mother and I, and finally the rest of the family. We had decided to remain here permanently, but one never really knew. It always would depend on how things worked out. The voyage to America took one month, and we sailed on a ship called the *Re d'Italia*. We hit a number of storms during the crossing and my mother was very sick. I think I was the only one who did not get sick. When we first left our home town of Marsala we were supposed to go to the port city of Palermo, but one of us became ill on the train *en route* to the city. The conductor notified the authorities in Palermo who became so worried that we had the plague that they took us to the *lazzaretto*, a hospital where people with infectious diseases are confined. We stayed at the hospital for two or three days during which time the boat had left for America. Consequently, we returned to Marsala, to await the next boat to make the trip. The journey across the ocean was so rough that it alone could discourage anyone from returning. I remember that when we arrived at Ellis Island a number of inspectors came through and it took a few hours but then we left with my brother who lived in Williamsburg, Brooklyn, on Ellery Street. Most of the early years we lived in that same section which was largely Italian at that time.

In 1924, right after being accepted to the bar I was married and for a year we lived in East New York in a rented apartment. Then I started to make a little money and we bought a one family house with three lots on Chestnut Street. At this time I became very active in law and in organizations of lawyers.

While the Italians stayed together, there was a tendency to gravitate toward people from the same area of Italy. There were so many of us from my home town of Marsala, some three to four hundred, that we tended to stay together in this circle. The Italians from different sections got along with one another, although it was different with other nationalities like the Irish. I remember going to a movie one day when I was about 14 and the kids started to holler at me, words like "wop" and "guinea" and then they threw stones. The Irish were prejudiced against the Italians and they thought themselves superior to the Italians because they knew the language and controlled the politics.

We did not have a real Italian judge until after World War I when Judge Sabbatino was elected. There previously was a Judge Rapallo but his family came to the United States so long ago that he was not really part of the Italian colony. Some 35-40 years ago we formed an Italian society called the Rapallo Lawyers' Association, and Miss Rapallo, a granddaughter of the Judge was there as a member. Judge Sabbatino's brother, Peter Sabbatino convinced us to name the association after Rapallo and the organization flourished and lasted for fifteen years. With the Second World War, however, it began to lose support and is no longer functioning. I was the treasurer of the association and Peter Sabbatino the president. Most of the Italian American judges in New York were members.

After having done extensive reading on my own, I had become a lawyer. At the time law school was only three years of preparation, whereas to become a doctor it would take much longer. My family encouraged me, but the cost was also lower then (about $100.00 a year). A friend of mine, who was the city editor for the *Corriere d'America* spoke in my behalf to the elder Luigi Barzini, and helped me to get a job translating some of the news which came over the wires. While working for them for three or four years, my father also encouraged me to learn how to barber so I could work weekends to supplement my income.

One of my closest involvements with Italian American organizations was with the Independent Order of the Sons of Italy. At that time I had a friend who was a member of the San Guiliani lodge in Brooklyn (lodges were usually named after a great man or a town), who advised me that since I was going to be a lawyer it would be to my benefit to join the Order. In 1921 or 1922, I was introduced and I became a member of the organization where I did meet people and gain clients. Of course I was then young and personable. I also gave lectures which helped to promote me to a position of importance in one of the district lodges. Thus, I supervised several lodges, meeting people and making contacts. Eventually, I was appointed Assistant Grand Venerable of the state. When Dr. Perillo died, I was named to his place and was re-elected to the post of Grand Venerable for 10 years in the Independent Order of the Sons of Italy. The Independent Order had broken off from the Sons of Italy around 1914 long before I became involved. For 10 years I served as Grand Venerable and was active for about 15 years altogether. After that, for no particular reason, I did not bother with it much anymore. Now, most of the Sons of Italy chapters around Long Island are of the Regular Order of the Sons of Italy. Whether the Independent Orders are still around I really do not know since I have not kept up with developments. While I was active I travelled in many lodges in New Jersey and Pennsylvania. For the most part, however, I was a deputy over a number of lodges in the Brooklyn area where I made many friends.

Regarding religious services, I must say my family was not very religious on a regular basis. For some reason we were lax then and even today my children are much more active in the church than I am. I was married in Our Lady of Loretto, a church in East New York which is still standing. At that time, of course, the parish was largely Italian. The priest there, Fr. Sala, was a good friend of mine with whom I used to go to political meetings. He may have been related to Judge Roland Sala, but I do not know.

There were a number of labor leaders in Brooklyn who came from Sicily. One was Judge Roland Sala's father who was a socialist and a radical. There was also Frank Bellanca and Luigi Antonini. We had a socialist club which we called the Avanti Club on Bushwick Avenue and Meserole Street. I delivered many lectures at this club and Roland Sala's father also frequented the place.

In the East New York neighborhood in which I lived I naturally became familiar with many Jews. In fact, I shared office facilities with Jewish lawyers where I was the only Italian. My wife's brother married a Jewish girl.

During the LaGuardia period I was also active in politics making many speeches over the radio in his behalf when he was running for mayor in 1933. The only thing he ever offered me after election, however, was the position of assistant corporation counsel. I, however, had hoped he would make me a magistrate as indeed many friends of mine thought he would. The job of assistant corporation counsel payed less than $3,000.00 a year and they said I could not practice law if I took the job. I thought, however, that if I could not even hang up my shingle and practice law, I could not possibly live on the assistant corporation counsel salary. I wrote a letter turning down the offer because I would stand to lose my practice for a low-paying job even if it were a high sounding title. Many people importuned LaGuardia on my behalf but nothing ever came of it. I also ran for the position of alderman once on the same ticket with LaGuardia but I lost by 1,000 votes. LaGuardia was of course a fiery individual and a major attraction among the Italian Americans in New York. He was like an idol.

I once had an interesting experience with LaGuardia. The Independent Order of the Sons of Italy had named a Bronx lodge, the Fiorello H. LaGuardia Lodge in his honor, and Edward Corsi was one of the leaders. Corsi had also tried to intercede with LaGuardia in my behalf. When LaGuardia first ran for the office of mayor in 1929 and was defeated by Jimmy Walker, the Regular Sons of Italy Lodge had, even though LaGuardia had been a member of that organization, supported Walker. The Independent Order of the Sons of Italy, however, had fully supported LaGuardia. There are a number of editorials and pictures in his behalf in our journals. One night we had a banquet shortly before he was elected mayor. I remember a speech in which he said "I have waited all these years, (for the chance to run for mayor) and to think the Independent Order of the Sons of Italy and this young man Rosario Ingargiola here supported me, while the other Order of the Sons of Italy, they were the 'Sons of Bitches' ". The Regular Order of the Sons of Italy were Democrats and did not support LaGuardia, while the Independent Order of the Sons of Italy fully backed him because he was Italian. We did not give a damn whether he was Republican or Democrat, the important thing was that he was an Italian.

Vito Marcantonio was a devoted supporter of LaGuardia working with him in the organization that Corsi created called the Harlem House. Marcantonio was a nice fellow but when he started associating with Communists, I lost all interest in him. I knew him when he was a Republican. He and LaGuardia first ran as Republicans, and it was only later that Marcantonio became a Communist. Nevertheless, we had been very good friends. He and Corsi would often come to our state conventions. A fellow like Marcantonio was very much involved with Italians, especially then when he had to depend on the Italians. After all, he could not expect to see Jewish clients coming to him as a lawyer. He became well known as did Sabbatino and a few others but, generally, young lawyers practiced most among their own ethnic group. When Marcantonio became more radical he was still supported by East Harlem's Italians but not so solidly as before, as even some of his earlier and closer friends such as Corsi backed off.

Edward Corsi was a gentleman. He knew Italian as well as I do, since his father had been an Italian deputy and a member of the Italian parliament who came here as an exile when Edward was just a young man. Edward Corsi was a very learned fellow, quiet and unassuming. He delivered a nice speech but he was not fiery like Marcantonio who could stir crowds. Corsi was sensible and held important positions such as Commissioner of Immigration. I remember that when he went to Europe as a correspondent for the *New York World*, right after World War I, he relinquished the column he had in *La Follia* which I then began to write. He and his wife both came to our conventions. When he ran for office we supported him and I made some speeches in his behalf, but he could not win as a Republican in the city of New York. He was on the liberal side, however, because of the background of his father. There was a weekly Sicilian American newspaper called *La Settimana Illustrata*, which was edited by his father. After his father died, Edward Corsi became editor of *La Settimana* which lasted only a few years longer. It had a following in New York, however, since most of the Italians here were from Sicily.

I remember the 1950 mayoralty elections in which all three main candidates were Italians. They were Edward Corsi, Vincent Impellitteri and Ferdinand Pecora. Impellitteri won the election, but it was a freak. He was not much of a mayor, although I did come to support him. At least he was on the human side and did not appear to be so arrogant as Pecora. By contrast, Impellitteri was more simple. He was not trying to put on airs or act as a great statesman.

The articles I wrote for *La Follia*, *Atlantica* and *La Lucerna*, were done *gratis*. The Sisca family published *La Follia*, while the publisher of *Atlantica* was a doctor named Casola. He got the idea of establishing a journal called *Atlantica* even though he was not a writer. From this whim he began a publication which lasted for about 10 years. Casola had a young fellow named Lamonica who was a kind of editor. Dr. Casola knew that I was writing for *La Follia*, and other newspapers and he used to call me up and ask me to come down and write for them also. At this point I was making a good living as a lawyer and I did not need any money, but writing was my hobby and I was anxious to write. I did not write for the *Vigo Press* which was published by John Schiavo who was a very good friend of mine. He came from Italy and became the pioneer historian of Italian American history, writing a number of books on the subject. I do not know how he did it because he did not have a good knowledge of English. He came here as a young man and had to learn the language but he was very ambitious and spent a lot of time in the library.

I also wrote for *Il Carroccio* and I still have a few copies. They published a work I did about 60 years ago. It happened that the Italian group at the City College of New York had a contest for an essay on Italian literature. I was lucky enough to win the prize and *Il Carroccio* published the essay. Agostino De Biasi, the editor of *Il Carroccio,* was a great writer, and a prolix one, often writing ten page editorials without any difficulty. He was a strong fascist, but he could certainly write. Unfortunately, good Italian publications in this country did not have much of an audience. Today, there are very few who read Italian anymore. The younger brother, Carlo De Biasi, started *Il Crociato,* an Italian Catholic newspaper in Brooklyn. Bruno De Biasi was a doctor. Agostino came to this country from Milano where he had been an editor and writer for *Il Corriere della Sera.* Concentrating mostly on editing he did not write so much here. We got along very well.

In fact, a book of mine which I published some years back was printed in the *Il Carroccio* printing shop.

Carlo Tresca was a colorful Italian American leader who was involved in some intrigue. I remember reading his *Il Martello* and his visiting our club *Avanti*. He delivered a speech there, which was very critical towards radicals. Yet, later on, he became very arrogant. Originally he came here as a socialist exile. I used to read his writings in *Il Martello* and *La Cronaca Sovversivo*. My life was spent among the Italians and I know many of them who wrote newspapers and who were active. I remember Domenico Trombetta, who published *Il Grido della Stirpe*. He was a good friend of mine, but he was the exact opposite of Tresca. We were friendly with all of them. We had our Sons of Italy office on 2 Lafayette Street where the Italian bank is. This was also the same building where Trombetta had his office. On the top floor there was a restaurant and we would often meet there. He was a fascist nut and an agressive type.

In the fascist period, Italian Americans for the most part favored fascism, not actively but spiritually. They thought that Mussolini was doing a good job and that he was straightening out the country, and providing order. Look at Italy now, it is ridiculous. If Mussolini had not taken sides with the Germans he would have been remembered as the greatest man in the world today. Up until then, however, he had been doing well. I was an American and I tended to look at Italy then from a distance. I looked upon Mussolini as a good man and I do think he was doing all right. True, some people were being persecuted, but you have to have a strong man for the Italians. They are so volatile for goodness sake! I read *Il Progresso* every Sunday, and it causes me to wonder about Italy. How many parties there are! There is going to be bankruptcy there soon and they need a fellow like Mussolini. The times have changed too much for that, but nevertheless a strong man is needed there.

During World War I a number of Italians in America went back home to support their home country. These were people who had not become Americanized and still regarded Italy as their motherland. During the Second World War it was different. Many of the Italians in America then were born here and so were their children. They could not fight against America. Moreover, Italian Americans were not enamoured of the Germans with whom Italy was now allied.

Crime was not so widespread then as the popular image portrays. Most crime among Italian Americans were crimes of passion and fights. There were a few criminals, and robbers, but the business about the mafia is bunk. In Italy they have organized groups of underworld gangs, but it was not that big here. The only thing I remember was *La Mano Nera* (the Black Hand). Organized crime started during the Depression and Prohibition. *La Mano Nera* was small-time stuff and it was not organized.

Regarding my final impressions about the immigrant experience I can say this is the greatest country in the world. There are no words to describe it. I came from Europe without much money, with no friends and with no knowledge of the language, as a kid. Eight years later I was a lawyer. I would say to these critics who villify this country that they could not succeed like that elsewhere and certainly not in Italy. In Italy, if you wanted to become a lawyer or doctor your father had to be a millionaire. Those from humble backgrounds could never rise to such heights in that society. Here, however, it could and did happen. Golden was right, "Only in America". I am only one small example but there are millions of others. All those who became fine lawyers and judges: Sabbatino, Caponegro, Liotta, Benevigna. Would they have been judges in Italy? Here they became outstanding judges. I have been practicing for 52 years and cannot recall any discrimination against me. This is the greatest country in the world.

Now, I am 78 years old and still do occasional work although I formally retired 14 years ago and got out of the rat race. I no longer go to court but I do still handle other matters for former clients and earn a little money for the children and grandchildren.

Elvira Adorno (signature)

*M*y father was born in Palermo, Italy. At nine years of age he ran away from home since he was second-born in the system of primogeniture. His brother Giuseppe was the first born. The system of primogeniture as it was in Sicily placed a terrible burden on the rest of the family. That is the first born son had to be well-dressed and present the *bella figura* while the other children worked his share in addition to their own. My father had to work hard as did his brother Basilio; by the time he arrived at school he would fall asleep at his desk. The teacher would call my father's home complaining about this for which his father would turn and slap him. After several doses of this punishment papa had enough and ran away.

At nine years of age, he became a cabin boy and he remained with the Marina Italiana about 20 years. He was auto-didactic, teaching himself how to add sums and read. He spoke so well, inf act, that later he became the orator for the *Ordine dei Figli d'Italia* (Sons of Italy).

The Adornos were natives of Genoa. When Italy became united it needed help to set up the new municipalities in the southern part of Italy. My grandfather was one of those sent to set up the new government. Probably because of that influence my uncle Giuseppe became chief of police and I think my dad, with his interest in politics and his love for speaking and writing, could have become a senator had he been able to continue his education.

After being at sea for twenty years, father wished to be on land again. He purchased a grocery shop and thought that one way of increasing his income would be to get orders from schools and orphanages. So he went to an orphanage and met the young woman who was in charge — my mother. Impressed with her ability, he fell in love and married her in 1900.

He had set up the grocery business during a weak economic period in Italy and it was difficult for anything to become profitable. Wanting to do much better for his family, he considered going back to sea; then again he didn't want to be away from his family. Finally, he decided he would go back with the Merchant Marine and jump ship after its arrival in the United States, which is exactly what he did. He settled in New York City and sought work as a presser in the clothing industry. This occurred during the early years of union organization and father attended every union meeting asking embarrassing questions regarding expenditures. Every time union members were assessed additional sums, he asked questions and requested to see the accountant's books. One day the union leadership approached him at his place of work telling him they wanted to make him a delegate. He looked at them and told them the offer was unexpected since they invariably shut him up at meetings. He understood that it was a bribe; in fact they told him that either he would become a delegate or they would "break his head". Not wanting to become part of this, he quit his job.

My mother did fine work in embroidery and crocheting, being especially expert at designs and filigree. Father reasoned that he would exploit this talent by going into business supplying Italian organizations in need of regalia and banners. Having saved some money, he sent for my mother and two brothers. They lived in Little Italy on MacDougal Street where I was born. This area was the only true Little Italy since people from the many regions were represented, whereas on Mulberry and Grand Streets, there were mostly Sicilians and Neapolitans. Strangely enough, more than 50 years after my birth on MacDougal Street, I went to teach graduate courses at New York University just a block away.

After quitting his job father started a flag and banner business and we moved to 212 Grand Street, a tiny railroad apartment that did not have its own bathroom. Mother helped father in his business; she was his only embroideress. She would get up after he had fallen asleep to pick up where she had left off, thus finishing orders on the flags (standards) on time. Central heating was unheard of in these buildings; my mother caught pleurisy, and died leaving father with four children. The authorities declared that since father had to go out to work, he could not take care of his children, and they would have to be put in orphanages: Alfred and Guy in one, and my little brother Joseph and I in another. Joseph died in the orphanage. Not wanting further separation, father decided to marry again. His mother in Sicily knew of a woman named Sandra, who was nearly 42, unmarried, and an embroideress. A correspondence between my father and my future stepmother began. The wife of the couple Sandra was living with in Sicily, Rosa Artale, was also an embroideress. Father paid the expenses for all of them to come to the United States. Poor Sandra Piccoli, a small frail woman who knew nothing of America or men, now arrived and assumed the running of a household including a husband and three children. In Italy she had lived a much easier life, where, although she worked she did not have to cook, clean or wash clothes.

Father's store was at 201 Grand Street west of Mott Street and we lived between Mott and Elizabeth Streets at 212 Grand Street. After the marriage, father moved us all to 207 Grand Street which had a big apartment. It had a tremendous living room which could be used as father's workshop. These banners were easily 6 feet wide and practically as long. Consequently, very large frames were needed. The frames, 7 feet by 7 feet in size, were made of oak placed on horses. Four women would be working on these frames at once. On the weekend these banners would be put up against the wall so we could use our big living room.

Around 1913, father named his firm the Adorno Flag Company, a simple name which was typical of flag business names. On the same block, there was the LaForte Flag Company which was close to Elizabeth Street. Two blocks further down toward Lafayette and Mulberry was the Di Caro Flag Company and practically next door to it was the Angelo Flag Company, which came in about ten years later. The concentration of flag companies on Grand Street probably caused father to move from MacDougal Street. The apartment at 207, eventually got too small so he rented the apartment upstairs too; he had two apartments in the same building before 1922.

Altogether there were four or five flag companies in the same area. Not only did these companies wait for customers to come in, but the owners also went to get business. Father, for example, was invited to demonstrate his wares as far west as Illinois. One of his original carrying cases was about a yard square; he had designed four or five display standards about that size, complete with poles. People used to come from Massachusetts, Connecticut, and from many areas where there were Italian American groups, clubs, or Little Italies which needed buttons, regalia, sashes or banners. It was quite a business since there were five companies on the same block; a prospective customer from out of state would shop around rather than take the first estimate. Father realized it was not to the benefit of the flag companies to cut each other's profits, so he formed a consortium. Thus, as soon as one company would receive a delegation, it would inform the other flag companies of the set price. For example, if the first price quoted was $1,200 the other companies would not quote a lower one. The company which received the job would then take ten to fifteen percent of the amount and put it into a fund which the companies would divide periodically. This then provided a source of money upon which they could all depend. Since papa was a capable talker and a good salesman, he usually wound up with the highest price and the order. Even though another flag maker would offer a $1,200 price, sometimes father got more for the same job.

In 1922, father did not want us to continue living in the city. In the summer he would send mother, my sister Addy and me for two or three weeks to his cousin's home in Bensonhurst, Brooklyn. There, mother would take us to a beach called Poverty Beach (where the V.A. Hospital and Belt Parkway are now located). Father thought the fresh air would do us good. He also used to send us to South Beach on Staten Island for a week or two. Eventually, he bought a two-family house on 16th Avenue and 76th Street in Brooklyn. It cost $16,000 in 1922 and was a beautiful house. There was a mixture of Italians and Jews in Bensonhurst.

When we were living on Grand Street, all of us went to P.S. 21, the old John Doty School in Manhattan. The principal was Anthony Pugliese. The Board of Education then was not so blind as some people thought because there was a principal of Italian background for the area. Angelo Patri was principal in the East Harlem area; so was Dr. Leonard Covello. I remember my 8th grade teacher was Mr. Canale who knew by brother Alfred and my brother Guy. Last year I took a group of adult students who studied Italian with me, for a visit to Little Italy. During the trip I thought I should go visit my public school; it had been torn down to make room for a new senior citizen center.

In the twenties, P.S. 21 had a rapid advance class, which meant you could do one year in half a year. One day they sent me home with a note for papa who wondered why they would want to do this. I explained that it would mean that I would go from 7A to 8A and skip 7B. Daddy said, "And what happens to all the things you were supposed to study in 7B?" I replied that I did not know. He said, "No, I won't give you that permission". He could not see why I should graduate at 12 years of age instead of 13.

As a child I was anemic; I think that this influenced the decision to move from Manhattan to Brooklyn. Papa felt the air would be better for me there. Since I did not like to eat much meat in those days, they used to give me beef tea. What a waste of money for the good meat was thrown away, and the tea alone would be drunk.

Both my brothers were artistic. Father, in the course of his work with the banners, would often have to use artists to design the sketches that he needed to present to the different societies for approval. He used to say to my brothers, "I don't want you to become artists".

In school, the teachers would naturally say how good they were at art. Consequently, both my brothers, without my Father's knowing (so they thought) would go to Cooper Union at night because they enjoyed doing this kind of work. Father still would not hear of either one of them becoming an artist. He wanted Alfred to become a lawyer, having bought a set of Blackstone legal books for him. At that time they did not have law schools as we know them. You studied your Blackstone and you went to take your exam. Alfred, however, was not interested. Papa said to Alfred one day, "You don't want to study? You either study or you are going to learn something practical". Next door to us at 207 Grand Street, was the De Natale jewelry family which had four sons. Papa spoke to Mr. De Natale, the Father, and said, "I'd like you to teach my boy Alfred to become an engraver". Mr. De Natale said sure, and it turned out fine since Alfred was artistic and readily took to engraving. It was another form of designing. Guy went to high school, but I do not think he ever finished. Papa needed him in the store, especially when he went out of town.

I remember one thing about World War I that impressed me a great deal. When the armistice for World War I was declared, some people from Washington, D.C. came to my Father's company to order flags that would span Constitution Avenue. They had been to the Anin Flag Company, the largest of this type of business in the city ordering a dozen or so flags of the allied nations. When the Anin Flag Company learned that these had to be completed in eleven or twelve days they said they could not do them in time because too much sewing was involved. The Washington men then went up Grand Street and tried Di Caro's who also turned them down. They then come to see dad who listened to them. As it happened, the year before he had bought a tremendous amount of material at a good price which he had stored in the rear of the high-ceiling store where he had constructed a storage platform. He realized he would need vast amounts of material. Looking at them, he asked how many days he had. "Eleven", they replied. Papa said, "I wonder if you can go out to lunch while I figure out if I can do them in time".

The men then went to the Villa Penza restaurant which is still in Little Italy. Father first decided that he had enough material to do the flags. Then he figured he could get my aunt, my step-mother, Mrs. Vaccaro and my uncle to help. The embroiderers also know how to use sewing machines. He told the men from Washington he would complete the flags for one thousand dollars each, a price agreeable to them. I remember distinctly the big living room we had in front of the two bedrooms. I remember the smell of the benzine which Father used in making the lines on the material to be cut. The whole operation left a strong benzine odor. My Father worked for two nights on a big table in the center of the living room cutting these tremendous flags. The one that gave him the most trouble was the English flag because of its large Union Jack.

Papa had calculated that he would need no more than two nights cutting the flag pieces, which were then sewn by the women who were situated throughout all the rooms of the house. He went back and forth through the rooms making certain that the work was done correctly. He was sensitive to the possibility of mistakes since some of the women had never sewn flags like these before. He gave the complex American and English flags to my mother, my aunt and Mrs. Vaccaro. The flags containing three panels were given to the other women to sew because they were simpler.

My Father realized that it would not be satisfactory to put up one solid piece of material across the avenue; a big wind could tear down the stanchions to which they were attached. The flags had to be made with openings which would allow the wind to pass through. He attached large metal grommets with heavy cords to tie the flags down. Thus, was he able to overcome the technical difficulties. As a result of this particular order, he was able to buy the $16,000 house in 1922. The entire job took eleven days: two nights to cut up the flag pieces and nine days of sewing.

By the time we moved to Brooklyn, my brother Alfred was an engraver, Guy was helping Papa, I was attending Bay Ridge High School and my sister Addy was going to the local elementary school. At the beginning of my junior year at Bay Ridge High School, New Utrecht High School opened. When Father heard that it was going to offer Italian he planned to have me transferred. In the meantime, I was majoring in Art without Father's knowledge. The art teacher wrote my Father not to transfer me since I was a good art student and might receive a Pratt Scholarship. My Father answered saying he wanted me to learn Italian and not art. "Artists starve!" The art chairman, however, made a strong point about the possibility of a scholarship. Father was still opposed to my majoring in art; hence I went to New Utrecht, studied Italian and was good at it which pleased father. At the new school I was invited into Arista, the honor society. In spite of the fact that I arrived at New Utrecht in my fifth term, I took three years of Italian in two years. I studied Italian during the summer on my own, taking tests in September thus advancing to the next class.

After high school in 1926, I went to Hunter College (knowing little about private schools). At that time Hunter had high entrance requirements. I majored in languages: French and Italian. I was allowed to take over 18 credits for a couple of terms permitting me to take two majors. Father's stubbornness regarding the study of Italian led to its becoming my livelihood later on. Italian became a major area of study because there were just enough students for it. Our professor of Italian, Dr. Ceroni, made sure every girl interested in Italian registered in his classes. He had a vested interest but I was thankful; most of our Italian courses, had to be in the evening to accommodate both day and evening students.

The flag business continued until the Depression in 1930 when Papa went bankrupt, at which time I graduated from Hunter and went to look for a job. I answered an ad for a saleslady job at Macy's and was met by a long line down around the block; I stayed on the line and advanced to the actual interview area. At that point I remembered my father's response to his *compare* who suggested I learn how to use a sewing machine instead of studying French and Italian. He informed his friend that since I was always interested in books I should be encouraged to study and not work in a factory. "I want her to be anything but a factory worker. If she's interested in languages, she's going to take languages." His friends used to ridicule this aspect of my education. The irony was, however, Macy's needed someone in the book department who knew languages. Consequently, I got my first job and went into the foreign book department in Macy's staying there for seven years.

Upon reflection, there was something about the Hunter College system that was discriminatory. You had to have close to an A or 4.0 average to take methodology courses. Every student should have had the opportunity to take them. The ones I took for teaching were most helpful, which qualified me to take the New York City teacher's exam. In 1930, I graduated from Hunter but was not able to take the test for teaching in New York City until six years later. In fact teachers had either lost their jobs or their salaries had been reduced at that time. As a result, many years went by before tests were announced for language teachers. In 1936 I took the one that was given for Italian, passed it and was assigned immediately because there was a need.

Many of the people teaching Italian had been substitutes.

After my father's business went bankrupt, he left the house and went to live with my aunt. I suppose it was the trauma of bankruptcy and failure. At twenty-seven years old, I became head of the household. Taking care of my mother, sister and my brother. During this time, real estate was going to pieces; people were losing their homes and renting. In fact I was unable to pay the mortgage for I was making only 24 or 25 dollars a week at Macy's. I did not want my sister to go to work insisting that she go to Brooklyn College despite the fact that these were bad times.

When my brother Guy got a job, he went to live with father. I do not think he liked my stepmother; I did not know why since she loved all of us. She never spoke badly of anyone. I remember once when I was a child a woman asked, "Does your mother treat you nicely?" I did not know how to answer the question because I did not know what she was talking about. I went upstairs and mentioned it to the ladies working on the banners, who had been with us for a long time; it was they who told me that I had a stepmother, and that my real mother had died of pleurisy. When we lived on Grand Street, I used to wonder who this lady was with the red hair in the oil painting above my bed; she was my mother. I used to wonder why the artist painted this lady with such red hair. It was in fact her natural color.

When I was a student in New Utrecht High School, our Italian teacher was Angelina Seveso. After graduation, at the beginning of each term at N.U.H.S. I would cover her Italian classes during her assigment to the program committee. It was a wonderful experience for me. In fact, one day when I was covering her class the principal Dr. Leuchs came in to observe, stayed the whole period and was pleased with my work. When he checked to see who I was, he discovered I was a former graduate of N.U.H.S.

The Italian Club at that school remained active even after our graduation. On one of the members' visits to our house, father said to me "Why do you young people waste your time skating and dancing? Why not form a club and be active in the community; you should know something about people running for office." So we formed the BIACL (Brooklyn Italian-American Civic League). We were in our twenties. Others joined including Anita Ligorio who was connected with a local radio station. We had done our homework, having found out the candidates running for office, presenting their views to the group. As a result of the BIACL, one of the club presidents, Larry Vetrano, was tapped by a local Republican group. Consequently he entered the court system and is now a judge, the only one of the group who made a name for himself through the club. Larry was preparing to become a lawyer and the men thought it was fine for a young Italian American to be interested in politics; that was the beginning of his career. In the late thirties I was teaching at Benjamin Franklin High School in East Harlem where we had evening meetings practically every week because the principal, Dr. Leonard Covello, was deeply involved with the community. At these meetings, the Italian American teachers were particularly involved. First, Dr. Covello took up the housing issue, with which the community worked to emphasize the need for improved housing for the area. The teachers helped in various ways such as mimeographing and distributing material. I was also in charge of one or two parties sponsored by the school which were intended to insure the success of some particular project Dr. Covello was involved in at the time. The building of a new high school was one of his projects; once the community got behind it with the dynamic leadership of Dr. Covello, it came to pass. Congressman Vito Marcantonio used to come to speak to the community groups; it seemed to me that he made the same speech repeatedly.

East Harlem was always a vibrant community where something was always going on. For example, on one occasion we had an affair in the gym which could take up to five hundred persons. The occasion was a fund-raising bazaar. I was called upon to decorate the gym. I had not yet learned that one had to use fire-proof paper. After it was up I learned about fire-proofing but it was too much to take down so I instructed students to go around during the evening to see that no one smoked.

I taught at Benjamin Franklin H.S. from 1937 to 1946, then transferred to Grover Cleveland in Queens where I taught Italian and another language. At this school there was not active Italian Club, although the study of Italian went along smoothly. In reviewing my educational career I really am grateful for Papa's insistence on my studying Italian. It insured my career in the field; in 1951 I received a Fulbright Scholarship to study in Florence, Italy.

The Italian Culture Council came about as a result of a decision of the Modern Languages Association in 1960, to put out a selected list of materials for various languages. Consequently, I was asked to be the national chairman preparing the list for Italian. After working on the project for a year, I came to the realization that there did not exist a place or an organization to which people could write to obtain information regarding the instruction of the Italian language and other facts on Italian Culture. In fact, prior to 1963, whenever the president of the American Association of Teachers of Italian received a request, he would send it to me for response. There were inquiries regarding how one could obtain a degree in Italian or questions regarding the use of some texts. Realizing the need for such a place where people could obtain information, I formed the Italian Culture Council. For seven years I wrote the bulletin which focused on providing useful information to teachers of Italian as well as exchanging and disseminating information about Italy and Italian Culture. These bulletins have since become basic source material.

Lately I am no longer active in the Italian Culture Council. I still receive requests for information but I am unable to put out any new bulletins; it was too much work and too expensive. Other groups have seen the need to publish similar material and are beginning to fill the gap. The American Association of Teachers of Italian has now started to fulfill much the same function.

Index